The Old Testament and the Literary Critic

L Cunningham

The Old Testament and the Literary Critic

by
David Robertson

FORTRESS PRESS
Philadelphia

For Jeannette

COPYRIGHT © 1977 BY FORTRESS PRESS

Library of Congress Catalog Card Number 76–62620
ISBN 0–8006–0463–6

Second printing 1982

9914G82   Printed in the United States of America   1–463

Contents

Editor's Foreword

The previous volumes in this series have introduced methods of biblical study which generally—though not always accurately—are considered to involve historical-critical perspectives. Most of these are exegetical methods, procedures involved in the interpretation of biblical texts. The exception is J. Maxwell Miller's *The Old Testament and the Historian,* in which the primary focus is not the interpretation of texts but the means of reconstructing the history of ancient Israel. The exegetical methods introduced in the series are historical-critical approaches in that they consider the biblical texts in relation to their historical contexts and recognize that every text itself has a history which should be analyzed. A caveat should be entered with respect to form criticism, for while it shares the assumption of historical-critical inquiry that the history of the biblical material should be investigated, it is best identified as a literary-sociological method because its interest is in the structure and genre of literary and oral language and it seeks to relate such language to recurring human situations or institutions.

The angle of vision on the Old Testament introduced in this volume is quite different from those treated in earlier volumes. The same material is investigated but on the basis of different questions and a distinct set of assumptions. Historical issues concerning ancient Israel or the biblical books themselves are steadfastly and intentionally ignored. The fundamental assumption, made at the outset as a self-conscious decision, is that the Old Testament is to be viewed as "pure" or imaginative literature, and thus studied as a contemporary literary critic would investigate the plays of Shakespeare or the novels of Sir Walter Scott. The "world" which interests the literary critic is that imaginative one created by the story or the poem. He does not ask how the story came together, or who Moses was, but takes the story as it stands and asks what role Moses plays in it, what the tensions and resolutions of the plot are. Furthermore, the "context" in which the Old Testament is considered is the vast body of human literature, potentially from the earliest times to the present.

The study of the Bible as literature is not new. Since the Enlightenment and the rise of historical criticism, scholars have considered it fundamental that, whatever else it may be, the Bible is a human book and is susceptible to study as other human books. And various forms of literary study have been applied in the twentieth century. But what is new is a growing awareness that not all criticism needs to be historical. The new seriousness about literary-critical work is part of that awareness; the application of various forms of structuralism to the Bible is another, often closely related, aspect of these different interests.

The term "literary criticism" has various meanings, and refers to different procedures. The goal of this book is to define the term and to illustrate some of the different ways literary critics investigate Old Testament literature. It is necessary at this point, however, to point out that "literary criticism" has been used frequently for what is more precisely designated as "source criticism." That is the method introduced in Norman Habel's *Literary Criticism of the Old Testament* in this series. Source criticism focuses upon literature—written documents—but its primary concern is with questions of date and authorship, and its major contribution is the recognition that many biblical works, for example the Pentateuch, should be attributed to more than one "author" or source.

The Old Testament and the Literary Critic introduces the assumptions, methods, and implications of literary-critical study of the Old Testament and then illustrates various aspects of the enterprise. Chapter II is an instance of the comparison and contrast of genres, in this case comedy and tragedy. The juxtaposition is heuristic: What would we learn about this text if we compared it with that one? Chapter III applies techniques for the study of rhetoric to an entire biblical book. Chapter IV looks at the aesthetic devices and internal dynamics of Psalm 90. The final chapter seeks to understand an important aspect of the poetic vision of the Bible as a whole.

GENE M. TUCKER

Emory University
Atlanta, Georgia
Winter, 1977

I

The Bible as Literature

Here are four varieties of written matter:

A struggle for existence inevitably follows from the high rate at which all organic beings tend to increase. Every being, which during its natural lifetime produces several eggs or seeds, must suffer destruction during some period of its life . . . otherwise, on the principle of geometrical increase, its numbers would quickly become so inordinately great that no country could support the product.

If evil has demonic or structural character limiting individual freedom, its conquest can come only by the opposite, the divine structure, that is, by what we have called a structure or "Gestalt" of grace.

The last government in the Western world to possess all the attributes of aristocracy in working condition took office in England in June of 1895. Great Britain was at the zenith of empire when the Conservatives won the General Election of that year, and the Cabinet they formed was her superb and resplendent image.

The door of Henry's lunch-room opened and two men came in. They sat down at the counter.
"What's yours?" George asked them.
"I don't know," one of the men said. "What do you want to eat, Al?"
"I don't know," said Al. "I don't know what I want to eat."
Outside it was getting dark. The street-light came on outside the window. The two men at the counter read the menu. From the other end of the counter Nick Adams watched them. He had been talking to George when they came in.

Even without a footnote identifying authors,[1] we recognize immediately that the passages are scientific talk, theological talk, historical talk, and literary talk, in that order. And along with identification comes a framework for evaluating each quote: a complicated network of assumptions about the kind of claims made by the text, the inten-

---

1. They are, respectively, Charles Darwin, *The Origin of Species* (New York: Collier Books, 1962), p. 78; Paul Tillich, *The Protestant Era* (Chicago: University of Chicago Press, 1948), p. xxi; Barbara W. Tuchman, *The Proud Tower* (New York: Bantam, 1967), p. 2; Ernest Hemingway, "The Killers," *The Nick Adams Stories* (New York: Bantam, 1973), p. 45.

tions of its author, the type of questions that should or should not be asked of it, the means of verification, and so forth. Now consider these texts from the Bible:

In the beginning God created the heavens and the earth. The earth was without form and void, and darkness was upon the face of the deep; and the Spirit of God was moving over the face of the waters. (Gen. 1:1–2)

Hear, O Israel: the LORD our God is one LORD; and you shall love the LORD your God with all your heart, and with all your soul, and with all your might. (Deut. 6:4–5)

And entering the tomb, they saw a young man sitting on the right side, dressed in a white robe; and they were amazed. And he said to them, "Do not be amazed; you seek Jesus of Nazareth, who was crucified. He has risen, he is not here; see the place where they laid him. But go, tell his disciples and Peter that he is going before you to Galilee; there you will see him, as he told you. And they went out and fled from the tomb; for trembling and astonishment had come upon them; and they said nothing to any one, for they were afraid. (Mark 16:5–8)

We cannot, I suspect, quite so readily identify the category of written matter these passages belong to. Much depends on our theological and critical presuppositions. Probably most of us are accustomed to understanding them as near relatives of one of the first three quotes above. And perhaps the single most important consideration in making up our minds is the intention of the passage in its original context. Succinctly put, to study the Bible as literature means to set aside these previous judgments, and, regardless of original intention, to consider not only these passages but the entire Bible in precisely the same framework and according to the exact same set of assumptions as we consider the quote from Hemingway. In other words, it means to consider the Bible, not as a variety of historical, or theological, or scientific talk, but as literary talk, and to ask of it the questions that are appropriate to literary talk. The purpose of this volume is to assist the reader in learning how to do this. In the four chapters that follow I will give my own literary reading of some selected biblical texts. In this chapter I want to discuss some presuppositions behind literary analysis in general and some of the implications of reading the Bible as a species of literature.

PURE AND APPLIED LITERATURE

Human beings like to tell stories and sing songs. Many, perhaps most, of these stories and songs have an immediate and fairly obvious utilitarian purpose: they are told by politicians, teachers, preachers, and parents to illustrate ideas and arouse emotions. Others, however, serve no apparent practical end; rather they seem to be uttered for

2

their own sake, for the pleasure of hearing a good story even if listening in no direct way helps solve any of life's more pressing problems. Since all of these stories and songs, whether utilitarian or nonutilitarian, are literature in the broad sense of the term, we customarily affix the adjective "pure" or "imaginative" when we want to distinguish the latter from the former. In this book the unmodified term "literature" always refers to the "pure" as opposed to the "applied" variety. Literary criticism refers to the conglomeration of procedures and manipulations people have invented to study imaginative literature; in an extended sense it also refers to the presuppositions underlying these procedures and the insights gained from their application. In short, literary criticism is the disciplinary study of pure literature, just as rhetoric is the methodological study of applied literature.

No one disputes that most of the Bible was originally written as applied literature: as history, liturgy, laws, preaching, and the like. To read the Bible as literature means that we cease to consider it under the rubric applied literature, and so no longer study it according to the procedures of rhetoric or history or theology; rather we take it as imaginative literature and begin to investigate it using the tools of literary criticism. I would like to be very clear on this point: reading the Bible as literature does not mean that we attempt to decide what texts, if any, were originally written as pure literature and make only these texts the objects of our literary investigations, while confining our remarks about other texts to literary devices used by their authors in accomplishing essentially nonliterary ends. Rather, we assume that the entire Bible is imaginative literature and study it accordingly. An analogy may help at this point. Works originally written as or commonly taken as pure literature (e.g., Shakespeare's plays, Keats's poems, Faulkner's novels) are, as it were, literary criticism's natural children. But other works (e.g., Donne's sermons, Gibbon's historical writings, Charles Wesley's hymns, and, of course, the Bible) may at some point in history come up for adoption. If adopted, they are treated (that is, analyzed) like natural children.[2] Now maybe the adoption will go well (as it has with Donne's sermons) or maybe it will go poorly (as it might if literary critics were to adopt, let's say, college textbooks). Can the Bible, the natural child of religion, find happiness in the literary critical household? I hope this book demonstrates that the answer is yes.

2. Compare, for example, the way historians often take a work of imaginative literature and study it as history, that is, as documentary evidence of the life and thought of a particular historical era.

The assumption that the Bible is imaginative literature is arbitrary. No one forces us to make it, nor does the Bible itself demand that we make it. We make it because we want to, because literary criticism can yield exciting and meaningful results. I also want to emphasize that consideration of the Bible as literature does not exhaust the possibilities for its interpretation, nor does it imply a negative judgment on other approaches. Literary criticism is not superior to alternative methodologies, just different.

To borrow a term from contemporary sociology of knowledge, we can call the shift from considering the Bible as applied literature to taking it as pure literature a paradigm change. Paradigm in this case refers to the set according to which a thing is considered, or the context in which it is placed for the purposes of understanding it and the procedures used within this context to investigate it. For example, Einstein's theory of special relativity is a paradigm for the study of motion different from that used in Newtonian physics, and the adoption by physicists of his formulas represents a paradigm change. The study of the Old Testament has already undergone at least three major paradigm changes. The first occurred when the Jewish people began to read it not simply as diverse writings in Hebrew but as scripture, as writings which, when taken as a whole, represent a canon of religious doctrine and practice. The second happened when Christians read it not as Jewish but as Christian scripture. The third, the shift brought about by modern critical investigation of the Bible, represented in one way a return to the first point of view, the Old Testament as applied writings in Hebrew; the new element was the study of it according to the criteria of critical historiography. Reading it as literature is now another and fourth major paradigm shift.

On each of these four occasions the Old Testament was wrenched fairly suddenly and none too gently from one context into another. From the point of view of those holding to a previous paradigm (for example, the Old Testament as Hebrew scripture) a new paradigm (for example, the Old Testament as Christian scripture) is arbitrary and entails a serious and even violent distortion of its original intention and true meaning. And, given the perspective out of which they speak, they are right. Considering Exodus 1–15 or the Gospel of Mark as literature will very likely, though not necessarily, involve a serious distortion of the original intention and meaning of these books as perceived by modern historical scholarship. Moreover, it seems unlikely that conflicting claims arising from divergent starting points can ever be arbitrated. This book is not the place to argue this most vexing philosophical issue. Suffice it to say here that literary critics are aware of the arbitrary nature of their starting point and are willing to sacrifice some goods, like the understanding of the Old Testament as given by critical historians, for other goods, the insights that will be gained only by considering it as literature.

LITERATURE AS METAPHOR

Literary criticism, like all sciences, is defined by the nature of the object it studies. The investigation of the motions of natural bodies calls for one set of methodological strategies, the investigation of human societies calls for different ones, and the study of imaginative literature[3] calls for yet others. Perhaps imaginative literature's most distinguishing characteristic is that it does not claim to describe reality itself but rather is a secondary reconstruction, an imitation of reality. Or, put another way, a work of imaginative literature creates another or alternative reality, analogous to the everyday world we live in, but not identical to it. We testify to this function of literature by labeling it "fiction."

That literature is an imitation of reality has some very significant implications. To begin with, it means that the building blocks of any work of literature are metaphors, just as history is made up of events, philosophy of ideas, and the real world of elementary particles. This statement does not mean that imaginative literature, more so than applied literature, makes use of various metaphoric devices, such as similes, tropes or figures of speech, conceits. Rather a more radical claim is made: everything in a work of literature, whether actions, dramatic personae, thoughts, or objects, is essentially metaphoric. Characters in a play are not real people but like real people; events in a novel are not the same as events in history but analogous to them. For example, Henry IV in Shakespeare's plays is not the real Henry IV; rather he is a fictitious character, and any reference to the real Henry IV in trying to estimate his character misses the point. His personality is to be understood solely in terms of the structure within which Shakespeare placed him. The irrelevance of an archaeological expedition to find the historical Hamlet in order better to understand Shakespeare's character illustrates the point. Or again, to use another famous example, Keats's claim in "Ode on a Grecian Urn" that "Beauty is truth, truth beauty" is a fictitious thought (that is, a thought occurring within a

3. For the purpose of defining literary criticism, only its natural children are, of course, considered.

fictive context) just as Henry IV is a fictitious character. The context for deciding its validity is the poem in which Keats places it, not, for example, the context in which a philosopher tests the validity of Plato's assertion that Truth, Goodness, and Beauty are one.

We are now in a position to be more specific about the nature of literary criticism: it is a disciplined investigation of written matter considered to be of its very nature metaphoric. It tries to answer such questions as, for example, how do you in practice arrive at an estimation of Hamlet's character, or how do you decide the validity of Keats's claim about Beauty. Of course, no precise recipes can be given. Fortunately, literary criticism is not an exact science; much depends upon the ingenuity of the individual critic. Nevertheless, some general guidelines can be laid down. First of all, the critic assumes, after any appropriate textual criticism is done, that the text he is interpreting is a whole, and that, while not every part of the text is of equal importance, every part is integral to the whole and each part modifies the meaning of the whole. Thus, a text is not interpreted until all parts have been brought into meaningful relation to the whole. Furthermore, the critic operates whenever possible by the principle of synecdoche, according to which a part stands for or equals the whole, and vice versa. That is, not only do all parts of a literary text stand in metaphoric relation to reality, but they stand in metaphoric relation to each other and to the work as a whole. Any portion of a literary text is like one of Leibniz's monads: it is distinct yet reflects the entire universe. Extremely clear examples of this principle come from the plays of Shakespeare, where, for instance, Hamlet's play staged for the benefit of the king metaphorically represents the play *Hamlet*, or where the actions of peasants comically mirror the more serious actions of the nobles.

How these guidelines might affect the interpretation of the Old Testament can be illustrated by considering the book of Genesis. To begin with, the text that the literary critic will find most interesting to study is the book as a whole. Because of the principle of synecdoche texts gain richness and complexity from having diverse, not easily assimilable, parts set in relation to one another. To dissect Genesis into J, E, and P and study these separately defies no sacred tenet of literary criticism; it is just less challenging and less exciting. Whatever the text, once it is chosen it is considered as if it were written by one author. If the entire book of Genesis is the text, then the fact that it was put together out of originally separate strands, if indeed it was, or that it went through several recensions, is of ancillary importance.

And certainly an attempt to solve structural or conceptual difficulties by relegating parts of the text to later redactors is a way of avoiding the interpretive enterprise. A thoroughgoing interpretation involves a consideration of all parts of the text, not only on their own but also in relation to each other. The meaning of the Joseph story (Gen. 37, 39–50), for example, depends as much on its relationship with the Abraham and Isaac stories (Gen. 12–36), the primeval history (Gen. 1–11) and Tamar's outwitting of Judah (Gen. 38) as it does on its own internal structure and language.[4] To understand the Joseph story as a microcosm mirroring by its form and content the macrocosm not only of the book of Genesis but also of the entire Bible is the goal of literary interpretation.

Because of its insistence that works of literature are wholes whose parts stand in metaphoric relation to one another, literary criticism, conceived of as a language, is more agglutinative than analytic. Along the way it may analyze, dissect, distinguish, but its final aim is always assimilative, inclusive. Use of this language, therefore, highlights tensions within texts, because inevitably many of the parts it wants to piece together will not mesh: they may be made of dissimilar materials, or have non-interlocking gears, or loose ends. (This is obviously true of a book by multiple authors, like the Bible, but it is also true of lyric poems like Shakespeare's sonnets, which are famous for the dissonances that reverberate between their parts.) Such tensions make the structure of literary works complex and ambiguous, giving their verbal texture richness and density. Scrutiny of these tensions and their effects (often called rhetorical criticism) has always been an important part of literary criticism, but it has been the hallmark of much criticism in the first half of this century. Critics like T. S. Eliot and I. A. Richards and their American followers have focused on such matters as subtleties and shifts in tone, paradoxes, uses of wit, and especially dramatic and verbal irony.[5] While the heyday of this type of criticism undoubtedly is past, it is safe to say that it will always occupy an important place in literary study of the Bible. The possibilities for irony are endless, as, say, the sacrifice of Isaac (Gen. 22) is set within the context, first, of the Abraham legends, then Genesis, then the Pentateuch, then the Old Testament, and finally the Bible as a whole.

4. See, e.g., Robert Alter, "A Literary Approach to the Bible," *Commentary* 60 (1975), 70–77.
5. For an example of this type of criticism, see Chapter III below.

CONVENTIONS AND GENRES

Because of literature's essentially metaphoric nature, it is like geometry in one crucial way, however different the two may be on scales that measure precision or connotation versus denotation: both are hypothetical and self-referential. That is, both involve the construction of imaginative universes that contain within themselves the rules and procedures by which they are to be interpreted. In one case these postulates may yield a world that corresponds quite closely to the world as we experience it in everyday life, where, let us say, space is not curved and parallel lines do not meet. Another set of postulates may yield, however, a world in which space is curved and parallel lines do meet. But in neither case does one prove theorems by consulting everyday experience or scientific experiments. Rather one proves theorems by referring to already established theorems that have been shown to follow from the postulates laid down in the beginning.

A writer proceeds in a way analogous to that of the geometrist. He too constructs a world according to postulates, although he rarely if ever states them explicitly. The literary critic calls these postulates conventions. Some conventions yield a world closely approximating our everyday world, as in a naturalistic novel by Dreiser. Others, as in fairy tales and science fiction, yield enchanting or bizarre worlds. But in every case we as readers make sense of these worlds not by reference to everyday life but by means of their controlling conventions. We do not, for example, base our response to talking frogs in a fairy tale, to heroes with magical powers in romances, or to gods talking with men in epics by consulting our everyday experience on these matters. One of the conventions of fairy tales is that animals can speak human languages. Once clues in the text (like "once upon a time") indicate to us that we are reading a fairy tale, we react to a talking frog in terms of the postulates of the story. This same principle holds, though with a twist, in the most "realistic" of all literary forms, the novel. One of the important conventions of the traditional novel is that its imitation of reality should appear to be very accurate, so that its people and events should look to us like people and events in our everyday life. Paradoxically, then, to read a novel according to its conventions we must look to our own personal experience of the world.

Of course, conventions are effective in governing our response because they are conventional, that is, traditional or standard ways of constructing a literary world and setting it in motion. Hence, the study of them by the literary critic is necessarily relational. Works that employ identical or similar conventions are said to belong to the same genre.[6] The scope of any particular investigation of genre, or the attempt to chart similarities and differences within any given sample of literary works (the process is similar to the division of plants and animals into species, genus, family, etc.), may be quite narrow or very broad. For example, the sample may be hymns in the Old Testament, or it may be hymns in the ancient Near East, or all hymns from whatever time and whatever place, or all lyric poems, of which genus hymn is a species, or all poetry, the family to which lyric poetry belongs. In other words, genre study, broadly understood, involves placing a work of literature within ever larger relational contexts until the context is all of literature, conceived as one vast body extending backward and forward in time and in all directions of the compass. To think of literature in this way is to do nothing more than follow to its logical conclusion the view of literature as essentially metaphorical. It stands in metaphorical relation to reality, and so altogether is a separate and meaningful whole or body, whose various parts are metaphorically related to each other.

To sum up this discussion of conventions, then, we can say that a work of literature is a hypothetical world, the clues for the understanding of which come from within the work itself. These clues, however, can be understood only by reference to the genre to which the work belongs. Therefore, we arrive at the conclusion that the decisive clues for interpreting any piece of literature come from other works of literature. Which other works one considers depends on the context used to determine the genre of the piece of literature in question. To consider the Bible as literature, then, means to incorporate it within the vast body of literature as a whole and to study its relationship with the other parts of that body. To consider a work within the Bible as literature involves determination of genre and interpretation according to the conventions of that genre.[7]

An important, albeit vexing, aspect of literary criticism is the arbitrary nature of the choice of context for determining genre. There is no a priori literary reason for preferring one context over another. One critic may wish to study biblical hymns in the context of the ancient Near East, another may choose all hymns in the Western literary tradition from Moses to Harry Emerson Fosdick. To those who have approached the Bible from an historical perspective the former

6. Gene M. Tucker, in his *Form Criticism of the Old Testament* (Philadelphia: Fortress, 1971), discusses generic studies of the Old Testament in a context more familiar to students of the Bible.

7. See Chapter II below for an example of this type of criticism.

may seem the obviously superior choice, but from a standpoint within literary criticism such a value judgment cannot be defended. All contexts are equally valid. Not all contexts, however, yield results that are of equal interest to the critic or his audience. Given modern civilization's preoccupation with history, a contemporary audience will likely be more excited by a literary study of biblical hymns in relation to Mesopotamian hymns than one comparing the Psalter with the Methodist Hymnal. And, in light of the escalating interest in Eastern religions, a reasonable surmise would be that future audiences will avidly read literary studies comparing the psalms with Vedic hymns. Without question, one of the handsome dividends of literary study of the Bible is the meaningful connections that can be made between biblical texts and texts that have little or no connection in space and time with biblical culture.

THE NATURE OF LITERARY INTERPRETATION

Since interpretation depends on context, there can be no single literary interpretation of a biblical text. The interpretation of Job, for example, will vary according to whether it is considered a wisdom text from the ancient Near East, a Greek tragedy, a situation comedy, and so on. Given an historical approach, which generally assumes that the superior interpretation is the one most closely corresponding to the author's intentions, or to the original audience's understanding, the interpreter would first investigate the literary conventions available to author and audience. If those of Greek tragedy were not available and those of ancient Near Eastern wisdom literature were, that would decide the issue. If both were available, then a decision would be based on the overall adequacy of competing theories to account for the evidence. Given a literary approach, which assumes that the author's intention and the original audience's understanding are merely two among a host of possible reference points for determining meaning, a different procedure would be followed. The validity of an interpretation of Job as a Greek tragedy depends not at all on the availability to the author of Hellenic models, but on the presence in Job of conventions that function as conventions in Greek tragedy do. For example, Yahweh's appearance and Job's recantings may not, historically speaking, have been modeled on the recognition scene in Greek tragedies, but they may actually function as such. From a literary perspective, then, it becomes quite feasible, even likely, that Job can be quite convincingly interpreted as Greek tragedy and as an ancient Near Eastern wisdom text.

Here again we see that literary criticism is agglutinative. Two readings of a text that follow from alternative interpretative contexts are not mutually exclusive. And as the context becomes ever larger, interpretations that follow from more restrictive contexts are taken up and allowed to resonate within the larger chamber. The situation is exactly parallel to the growth of a text by accretion. Job without chapter 28, the Elihu and Yahweh speeches, has a meaning; as each of the above is added the meaning changes. The meaning of the book as a whole includes all the others, and is correspondingly all the more rich. And, of course, the same is true of the Bible as a whole, from its presumed beginnings as the Law of Moses to its present form. But not even by including the entire body of literature as the context for interpretation can a final, all-encompassing meaning be arrived at, for this body is always growing. New texts are added daily, and each one modifies, however slightly, the shape of the whole. The writing of *J.B.* changed the meaning of Job; the publication of Neil Simon's *God's Favorite* further changed it. In interpreting *J.B.* we naturally assume that we are to consider it in relation to Job, just as we consider O'Neill's *Mourning Becomes Electra* in relation to Sophocles' *Electra*. We do not so automatically reckon with *J.B.* when interpreting Job. But, in any comprehensive interpretation of Job we must do so. In the literary universe, unlike the real one, time runs both forward and backward.

QUESTIONS OF TRUTH

During the past two millennia the truth of the Bible has been an overriding concern among its interpreters. Does it tell the truth about events in Palestine from about 1200 B.C. to about 100 A.D.? Does it tell the truth about us and about God and about our relationship with him? The literary critic is also concerned with truth, but for him it has a rather different meaning. In most literary discussions, truth seems to mean something like "appropriateness." The correspondence of an event or an idea in a work of literature to some standard outside the work is irrelevant. Its "fit" within the world created by the work is what matters. And one measures its fit not by calipers or syllogisms but by sizing it up (inevitably a subjective procedure, a matter of perspective) in relation to other events or ideas in the same work. Let us take an example. Charles Dickens wrote two endings to *Great Expectations*, one in which boy does not get girl and one in which boy gets girl. It is nonsensical to ask which of these endings is true if truth means correspondence with events outside the book, for there

11

are in this case no such corresponding events. If, however, truth means appropriateness, then the truth question can be asked and intelligent answers given. In light of the conventions employed in the book, which ending better rounds out the story? Which ending is more consistent with the personalities of the protagonists and their histories?

The ending of Job provides a reasonably close parallel to *Great Expectations*. Does the return to the folk tale provide a suitable conclusion to the story? Or is the story more effectively told if it ends with verse 6 of chapter 42? Or, again, could verse 5 of chapter 40 be the most appropriate ending? Because Job is the most obviously literary book in the Bible, such questions are familiar to biblical critics. But they have not asked similar questions of the Gospel of Mark. Once it is taken as literature, however, they are the questions to ask. When Mark reports that the women find the tomb empty, the historian wants to know, was the tomb empty? The literary critic wants to know: given events up to that point, the character of Jesus, what he has said and done, does an empty tomb and a risen Jesus effectively complete the story? In other words, does the empty tomb motif symbolically and emotionally fulfill the action, in the way, for example, Oedipus' self-blinding fulfills the action of Sophocles' *Oedipus Tyrannus?* Or take a more problematic aspect of the conclusion of Mark, the report that the women were so afraid that they told no one of what they had seen. This is a curious detail; we are hardly prepared for it. Is it a flaw in the narrative? Would the story be more successful if the women had been overcome with joy and had run immediately to tell the disciples? Or, on the contrary, is our surprise at the women's silence a hint that we have not read Mark's story very carefully, and that we should reevaluate our interpretation of it in light of this strange detail? These are not easy questions to answer, but they are exciting, and the type of questions that will be asked once Mark is read as literature.

It follows from the above discussion that the accuracy of historical assertions made in a work of literature is completely irrelevant to a literary discussion of it. This statement is valid for Gibbons, for Shakespeare, for Truman Capote's *In Cold Blood* as well as for the Bible. And what is true for historical assertions is, of course, also true for theological claims. Having read John 3:16, "For God so loved the world that he gave his only Son, that whoever believes in him should not perish but have eternal life," the literary critic wants to know, not is there a god who sends his son to earth for our welfare, but are the symbols used in this verse (God, Son of God, divine mission, etc.) adequate to interpret the principal action of the story. If no god like the Lord of the New Testament exists, then John makes a theological claim that is false. The book does not, thereby, become less beautiful, just as the *Iliad* does not become less beautiful if Athena does not exist.

Having used the word beautiful, perhaps we can summarize the preceding paragraphs by saying that the literary critic's final concern is with Beauty, not Truth. For in defining truth as "appropriateness" we are speaking primarily of aesthetic qualities like internal harmony, consistency, being an integral part of a whole. From a literary point of view, at least, Plato's claim that Truth and Beauty are one is surely false.

THE VALUE OF LITERATURE

But what about the third member of Plato's trinity, the Good? What good does literature accomplish for those who read it, and more specifically, what good will proceed from our reading the Bible as literature? The value of literature has always been a vexing matter to literary critics. That it is valuable seems more or less apparent: many people spend hours reading it; publishing it is very big business; paperback editions are on sale wherever traffic is heavy, in grocery stores, drug stores, airplane and bus terminals, and the like. Yet to say with any precision what this value consists of is exceedingly difficult. The reason for this situation is not hard to find. We can relatively easily explain to ourselves the value of history, theology, and physics, for they attempt to describe as accurately as possible the world we live in. Literature, on the other hand, being an imitation of reality, has an indefinite and indirect bearing on our everyday world. It follows inevitably, I think, that its value to real people will also be indefinite and indirect.

Perhaps we can approach this problem by considering two meanings of the word "play." It is surely no accident that we say children imitating their parents "play," and call the performance of a drama "a play." One thing a child is certainly doing when she imitates her mother is practicing, practicing in anticipation of the time when she will be a mother for real. This practice involves the learning of emotional attitudes as well as physical skills and social routines. So, when the time comes for her actually to nurse her baby, discipline her child, or seek a job, she will have gone through the motions, and so know, in a sense, what it feels like. Reading a work of literature is also a kind of practice, differing from children's play only in that explicit motor responses are involved hardly at all. In other words, reading and the play of children are practice for living. This is one reason why all great literature is about the archetypal human situations, like growing up, learning to love, gaining, losing, dying.

Once again, let us take a classic example. Oedipus of Sophocles' tragedy is a representative human being. When we identify with him, all of our wonder at being alive wells up and, at the same time, all of our fear. In other words, we are playing at being human as we watch this play. As Oedipus blinds himself and is cast from the stage, we enact proleptically our own inevitable fate. He bears his fortune nobly. As we watch him, we practice how we will bear ours. Our wonder and our fear are contained in and by a state of acceptance of our humanness and its ultimate end; or, as Aristotle put it, the action of tragedy casts out fear and pity.

My point is put programmatically by Wallace Stevens in his poem "Of Modern Poetry":

> It [i.e., poetry] has
> To construct a new stage. It has to be on that stage
> And, like an insatiable actor, slowly and
> With meditation, speak words that in the ear,
> In the delicatest ear of the mind, repeat,
> Exactly, that which it wants to hear, at the sound
> Of which, an invisible audience listens,
> Not to the play, but to itself, expressed
> In an emotion as of two people, as of two
> Emotions becoming one.[8]

Even though Stevens is speaking directly about the relationship between author and book, what he says is also applicable to reader and book. Works of literature are like actors on a stage; readers of those works are like the audience. Reading is a process by which what happens in the work is internalized by the reader until reader and book become one. And the purpose of this union is to find the attitudes and emotions that will best help us live our lives: "modern poetry," says Stevens, and by extension we can understand this term to mean all imaginative literature, is "an act of the mind" finding "what will suffice," that is, what will enable us, hopefully, to live imaginatively.

In light of this quote from Stevens a statement made at the begin-

8. Wallace Stevens, *The Collected Poems of Wallace Stevens* (New York: Alfred A. Knopf, 1968), p. 240.

ning of this introduction now needs revising. There I contrasted pure with applied literature. Now it is clear that even pure literature has an end. It may not have immediate cash value, as it were, just as children's playing has no cash value. Nevertheless, viewed from the context of humanity as a whole, imaginative literature does serve an extraordinarily important function: the corpus of world literature can be viewed as authored by the human race as a means of practicing how to live, of finding what will suffice to make our lives meaningful and valuable.

What, then, is to be gained by reading the Bible as literature? Certainly, the Bible read as imaginative literature is a very different book from the Bible read as scripture. We cannot, therefore, expect it to deliver the same kind of goods it delivers when read as scripture. The difference between these two types of goods is well put by Robert Frost in his most celebrated statement about literature:

The figure a poem makes. It begins in delight and ends in wisdom. The figure is the same as for love. . . . It begins in delight, it inclines to the impulse, it assumes direction with the first line laid down, it runs a course of lucky events, and ends in a clarification of life—not necessarily a great clarification, such as sects and cults are founded on, but in a momentary stay against confusion.[9]

The Bible, taken as a receptacle, contains some of humanity's most beautiful speech. The Bible, taken as a single work of art, is one of the world's greatest books. As literature it loses none of its power; rather its power is of a different sort: finite instead of infinite, a power to aid rather than to save. It joins the likes of Homer's epics and Shakespeare's plays in literature's grand symphony of imaginative speech that offers temporary order, insight, and peace.

In this Introduction I have tried to lay out some basic presuppositions underlying a consideration of the Bible as literature. Now I want to put some flesh on these theoretical bones by analyzing as literature some selected biblical texts.

9. Robert Frost, "The Figure a Poem Makes," in *Selected Poems of Robert Frost* (New York: Holt, Rinehart and Winston, 1962), p. 2.

II

Comedy and Tragedy:
Exodus 1-15 and the Bacchae

As designations of genre the terms comedy and tragedy are met frequently in literary criticism. Sometimes they are used in a very broad sense to describe basic plot lines: a comedy is a work in which the hero is in the end incorporated into the society to which he properly belongs; a tragedy is a work in which the hero is in the end cast out of the society to which he properly belongs.[1] At other times they are used more narrowly to describe a family of works that are comic or tragic in the broader sense, like Greek or Elizabethan tragedy, old or new comedy. In this chapter I will try to show that, in terms of its plot line, Exodus 1-15 is a comedy: its two heroes, Moses and Yahweh, are integrated into the societies to which they rightfully belong. And, in order to gain a more precise understanding of the type of comedy Exodus 1-15 is, I will set it over against one particular Greek tragedy, Euripides' *The Bacchae*,[2] and argue that the two works are mirror images, the obverse and reverse of the same dramatic coin. Specifically, I think that the literary conventions that governed the writing of *The Bacchae* are also operative in Exodus 1-15. Since these conventions are used by Euripides to produce a tragedy and in Exodus 1-15 to produce a comedy, comparing the two works will allow us to isolate quite precisely the narrative manipulations that turn the same plot into, on the one hand, a tragedy, and on the other hand, a comedy. At the end of this chapter I will be concerned especially to note the effects of these manipulations on the attitudes and feelings of the audience/reader. When one practices living (see Chapter I) by read-

1. Compare especially Northrop Frye, *Anatomy of Criticism* (Princeton: Princeton University Press, 1957), third essay.
2. The translation used is by William Arrowsmith, *The Bacchae*, in *The Complete Greek Tragedies*, ed. David Grene and Richmond Lattimore (Chicago: University of Chicago Press, 1959), vol. V. Reprinted by permission of The University of Chicago Press.

ing Exodus 1–15, one learns quite different attitudes and experiences quite different emotions from when one reads *The Bacchae*.

In terms of the theory of literature outlined in Chapter I, several aspects of the literary analysis undertaken in this chapter are arbitrary. First is the choice of Greek drama as a context for interpreting Exodus 1–15. Certainly, historically speaking, the former exercised no influence on the composition of the latter. The choice is based solely on heuristic considerations: putting Exodus 1–15 over against *The Bacchae* produces some interesting results. Second is the decision to discuss Exodus 1–15 in its received form. Third, and finally, is the decision to take Exodus 1–15 (or to be more precise, Exodus 1–15:18) as a discrete unit. While the song sung by Moses and the Israelites in celebration of Yahweh's defeat of the Egyptians brings to a close one episode in the story of Moses, no convincing evidence exists to suggest that biblical authors or editors considered this episode isolatable from what follows. The decision to consider it in isolation results from the prior decision to study it in relation to Greek drama in general and *The Bacchae* in particular.

THE ESSENTIAL PLOT

Both *The Bacchae* and Exodus 1–15 tell the story of how a strange and little known god authenticates his claim to godhood by unleasing his divine power against a proud and stubborn unbeliever. In *The Bacchae* the god is Dionysus and the unbeliever is Pentheus, king of Thebes. Dionysus is the son of Zeus by the mortal Semele, Pentheus' aunt:

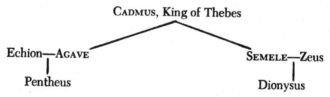

CADMUS, King of Thebes

Echion—AGAVE   SEMELE—Zeus

Pentheus   Dionysus

Hera, enraged by Zeus' extramarital affair, killed Semele with a mighty lightning blast, but the unborn Dionysus was rescued by Zeus and hidden in his own thigh until birth. Dionysus was first worshiped as a god in lands far to the east of Greece. From there he steadily made his way west, heading toward his homeland and making converts along the way. A hero's welcome for the local god made good, however, does not await him in Thebes, for the people there doubt that he is in fact a god. They say that Semele slept with a man, and that her father, Cadmus, to protect his daughter's honor, made up the story of her seduction by Zeus. Furthermore, Pentheus, Cadmus' grandson, is very upset by the reported licentiousness of the female followers of Dionysus, called Bacchae. He says, in his opening speech:

> I happened to be away, out of the city,
> but reports reached me of some strange mischief here,
> stories of our women leaving home to frisk
> in mock ecstasies among the thickets on the mountain,
> dancing in honor of the latest divinity,
> a certain Dionysus, whoever he may be!
> In their midst stand bowls brimming with wine.
> And then, one by one, the women wander off
> to hidden nooks where they serve the lusts of men. (lines 215–23)

The king is determined to act forcefully against the moral anarchy that threatens to tear apart the social fabric of his state. Dionysus, in order to demonstrate his divinity and also redeem the reputation of his followers, has disguised himself as a man, an Asian leader of the Bacchae, who in turn serve as the chorus in the play. In his opening speech Dionysus reveals himself to the audience and discloses his purpose:

> I am Dionysus, the son of Zeus,
> come back to Thebes, this land where I was born.
> . . . .
> And here I stand, a god incognito,
> disguised as man, beside the stream of Dirce
> and the waters of Ismenus.
> . . . .
> Like it or not, this city must learn its lesson:
> . . . .
> Cadmus the king has abdicated,
> leaving his throne and power to his grandson Pentheus;
> who now revolts against divinity, in me;
> thrusts me from his offerings; forgets my name
> in his prayers. Therefore I shall prove to him
> and every man in Thebes that I am god indeed.
> (lines 1–2, 4–6, 39, 43–48)

Pentheus thinks Dionysus, in his disguise, is some foreign lover boy intent on leading Theban women astray, and has decided to move against him:

> I am also told a foreigner has come to Thebes
> from Lydia, one of those charlatan magicians,
> with long yellow curls smelling of perfumes,
> with flushed cheeks and the spells of Aphrodite
> in his eyes. His days and nights he spends
> with women and girls, dangling before them the joys
> of initiation in his mysteries.
> But let me bring him underneath that roof
> and I'll stop his pounding with his wand and tossing
> his head. By god, I'll have his head cut off! (lines 233–41)

The stage is thus set for the momentous confrontation between wronged god and proud man.

In Exodus 1–15 the deity is Yahweh, the god of a group of obscure Semitic tribes. He lives on a mountain far to the east of Egypt, in the land of Midian, and it seems that he has been mostly absent from his people during the immediate past, for they do not even know his name. Thus, not only must he convince his opponent that he is a god worthy of the name, but his own followers as well. The opponent in question is Pharaoh, the tyrannical king of Egypt. Structurally, the first two chapters of Exodus accomplish three things: they explain the antagonism between the Israelites and Pharaoh, introduce us to the man who will serve as Yahweh's emissary to Pharaoh, and get Moses to Midian so that he can meet Yahweh. Israel's extraordinary population explosion has brought them to the attention of Pharaoh, who, frightened by their numbers, responds cleverly and cruelly: after the failure of his pact with the Hebrew midwives, he instructs his own people to kill all male Israelite children. We are then told how Pharaoh is outsmarted by a young Hebrew child, who manages not only safety for the baby but an Egyptian rearing and education! The necessity of flight after this Hebrew boy, now an adult, kills an Egyptian man is the mechanism used to get him to Midian.

Chapters 1–2 are also important thematically. The outwitting of Pharaoh by the Hebrew midwives and by Moses' sister foreshadows the climactic events of the story (as does Moses' murder of the Egyptian) and serves to orient us to the literary world we are entering, analogous to the way "once upon a time" introduces us to a fairy tale world. We learn right away that this story belongs to the genre of folk story in which clever stratagems by the oppressed enable them to triumph over the superior but unjust forces of the wicked. And these anticipations of later events help us to sort out our allegiances and prepare us emotionally for the denouement. We know who is going to win and even how they are going to win. We also know whom we want to win: stories with clear-cut moral themes tend to arouse clear-cut emotions, a strong sympathy for the weaker party and an intense antipathy toward the stronger. It is crucial that we do not in any way sympathize with Pharaoh, so pains are taken to present him in an uncomplimentary light from the very beginning.

Chapter 3 introduces us to Yahweh, god of the Israelites. As we expect, he is presented to us in a wholly good light. He is the defender of the poor and oppressed. He has seen his people's suffering at the hands of Pharaoh and is about to act. He himself suggests to

19

Moses the initial stratagem to be used against Pharaoh: the ruse of a round-trip journey into the desert. Yahweh, of course, actually has in mind a one-way trip to Palestine via Sinai. After telling Moses his name so that both the Israelites and the Egyptians will know with whom they are dealing, he gives Moses (chapter 4) the tools for bargaining with the more powerful Pharaoh: a magical wand and an eloquent brother. It is not surprising that Moses shows some hesitation in carrying out Yahweh's directives. A reticent hero is a typical convention of this type of folk story. He adds a welcome but quite tolerable tension to the story. Might Moses fail? Surely not . . . but maybe. Aaron enters as reinforcement. He too performs a stereotyped role: the hero's sidekick. But Aaron is never well integrated into the story, and just as well could be edited out. Once Moses has returned to Egypt and has met Aaron, we are prepared for the confrontation with Pharaoh.

THE AGON

Back now to *The Bacchae*. Its agon, or head-to-head contest between protagonist and antagonist, begins, as is often the case in Greek tragedy, as a battle of words. A servant brings Dionysus to Pentheus, and the two engage in about one hundred and fifty lines of rapid verbal fire. Pentheus begins:

> So,
> you are attractive, stranger, at least to women—
> . . . .
> Your curls are long. You do not wrestle, I take it.
> And what fair skin you have—you must take care of it—
> no daylight complexion; no, it comes from the night
> when you hunt Aphrodite with your beauty.
> . . . .
>   What form do they take,
> these mysteries of yours?
> D.   It is forbidden
> to tell the uninitiate.
> P.   Tell me the benefits
> that those who know your mysteries enjoy.
> D. I am forbidden to say. But they are worth knowing.
> P. Your answers are designed to make me curious.
> D.   No:
> our mysteries abhor an unbelieving man.
> P. You say you saw the god. What form did he assume?
> D. Whatever form he wished. The choice was his,
> not mine.
> P.   You evade the question.
> D.   Talk sense to a fool
> and he calls you foolish.
> . . . .

P.   Do you hold your rites
    during the day or night?
D.   Mostly by night.
    The darkness is well suited to devotion.
P.   Better suited to lechery and seducing women.
D.   You can find debauchery by daylight too.
P.   You shall regret these clever answers.
D.   And you,
    your stupid blasphemies.
P.   What a bold bacchant!
    You wrestle well—when it comes to words.
                    (lines 453, 455–58, 470–79, 484–90)

Pentheus at this point escalates the contest. He cuts off Dionysus' curls, seizes his magic wand, and then announces his intention to imprison the disguised god:

Last, I shall place you under guard and confine you
    in the palace.
D.   The god himself will set me free
    whenever I wish.
P.   You will be with your women in prison
    when you call on him for help.
D.   He is here now
    and sees what I endure from you.
P.   Where is he?
    I cannot see him.
D.   With me. Your blasphemies
    have made you blind.
P.   Seize him. He is mocking me
    and Thebes.
D.   I give you sober warning, fools:
    place no chains on me.
P.   But I say: chain him.
    And I am the stronger here.
D.   You do not know
    the limits of your strength. You do not know
    what you do. You do not know who you are. (lines 496–506)

It has by now become clear that Pentheus is an example of that figure so often met in Greek literature, the *alazon* or boaster, the man who thinks he knows more than he does know and who therefore assumes a higher place in the hierarchy of things than he is entitled to. And Dionysus incognito is quite literally the *eiron* or the one who, to expose the pretentious *alazon*, pretends to be less than he is and to know less than he knows.

Once in prison Dionysus unleashes his magical powers: an earthquake topples the castle and fire consumes it. Dionysus reappears and informs his followers that Pentheus never enchained him at all, for he substituted a bull for himself and watched bemused as Pentheus struggled to rope and tie it. Pentheus also reappears looking for

21

Dionysus. After more debate between the two a messenger arrives and describes the revels of the Theban women, led by Agave, Pentheus' mother, on the hills outside the city. Pentheus is mortified and vows to capture and punish the revelers. As he begins to don his armor, Dionysus lays his trap:

> Wait!
> Would you like to see their revels on the mountains?
> P. I would pay a great sum to see that sight.
> D. Why are you so passionately curious?
> P.   Of course
> I'd be sorry to see them drunk—
> D.   But for all your sorrow,
> you'd like very much to see them?
> P.   Yes, very much.
>   (lines 811–16)

Pentheus, it seems, is like the proverbial censor who publically rails at the evils of pornography but who secretly cherishes his place on the censor board because it allows him access to the material he denies to the general populace. Dionysus tells Pentheus that he must wear woman's clothes in order not to be detected. Pentheus hesitates at first, but, under the god's spell, finally agrees. After helping Pentheus dress, Dionysus makes great fun of him before the chorus by arranging his hair and straightening his hem. The two then leave for the hills. After a song by the chorus a messenger arrives and tells with excruciating detail how Pentheus was discovered by the Theban women and dismembered by none other than his own mother. Before considering *The Bacchae*'s emotionally wrenching recognition scene, let us once again return to Exodus.

The bulk of Exodus 1–15, like *The Bacchae*, narrates the agon, or contest, between protagonist Yahweh and antagonist Pharaoh, with Moses serving as intermediary. And here, also, the weapons are words and magic wands. In chapter 5 Moses and Aaron try to trick Pharaoh into letting the Israelites escape by requesting a leave of absence:

Afterwards Moses and Aaron went to Pharaoh and said, "Thus says the LORD, the God of Israel, 'Let my people go, that they may hold a feast to me in the wilderness.'" (5:1)

Pharaoh responds:

"Who is the LORD, that I would heed his voice and let Israel go? I do not know the LORD, and moreover I will not let Israel go." (5:2)

This reply is crucial, for it tells us what really is at issue in this contest: recognition by Pharaoh of Yahweh as a god, as the most powerful god, as god in Egypt as well as in Midian. Throughout the following chapters Yahweh will repeat his ultimate aim over and over to Moses

22

so that Moses can repeat it over and over to Pharaoh. That aim is not simply to free his people, for that could be done directly, without the attendant fanfare of the plagues. No, it is:

that you may know that there is none like me in all the earth. For by now I could have put forth my hand and struck you and your people with pestilence, and you would have been cut off from the earth; but for this purpose have I let you live, to show you my power, so that my name may be declared throughout all the earth. (9:14–16)

Moses and Aaron reply to Pharaoh:

The God of the Hebrews has met with us; let us go, we pray, a three days' journey into the wilderness, and sacrifice to the Lord our God, lest he fall upon us with pestilence or with the sword. (5:3)

In terms of what Yahweh had said previously to Moses about punishing Pharaoh, this is a very weak-kneed statement. Yahweh never said he would bring plague or sword on the Hebrews. Moses and Aaron, it seems, are unduly cautious in Pharaoh's presence. All they succeed in doing is making life more difficult for their people. Because of their failure of nerve Yahweh must repeat his self-revelation to Moses and renew his instructions (6:2–7:7).

Perhaps because of these disclosures, Moses introduces magic into his very next encounter with Pharaoh. But the mere performance of miracles does not constitute unequivocal evidence of Yahweh's supremacy over Egyptian gods, for the Egyptian magicians are also quite talented. So Yahweh must continue the plagues until they cannot duplicate his feats. We reach this point rather quickly, however. The Egyptian magicians can turn wands into snakes, water into blood, and produce frogs, but they cannot, for reasons that are not expressed, manufacture gnats. They point out to Pharaoh, "This is the finger of God" (8:19). Thus, insofar as plagues are used by Yahweh to convince Pharaoh that he is dealing with a god with power even in the land of Egypt, all plagues after the gnats are superfluous. More are included, it appears, partly to make Yahweh's power unmistakably impressive. But after their function as evidence of Yahweh's power has been fulfilled they continue for another and more important reason. They are scaffolding for Moses' negotiations with Pharaoh. For these negotiations to take place Moses needs to have a rather large number of audiences with Pharaoh. The plagues are an ideal mechanism to bring the two men together frequently, for each time Moses must announce a plague to Pharaoh and each time Pharaoh must summon Moses to ask that it be suspended. It is in these negotiations that the crucial contest between them occurs, the miracles serving as an indispensable prop.

Pharaoh makes his initial concession after the fourth plague: "Go, sacrifice to your God within the land" (8:25). Moses' reply is clever and to the point: "It would not be right to do so; for we shall sacrifice to the LORD our God offerings abominable to the Egyptians. If we sacrifice offerings abominable to the Egyptians before their eyes, will they not stone us? We must go three days' journey into the wilderness and sacrifice to the LORD our God" (8:26–27). Pharaoh concedes the point and makes a counter proposal: "I will let you go to sacrifice to the LORD your God in the wilderness; only you shall not go very far away" (8:28). Of course, they do not go at all. After three more plagues the strain is beginning to tell on Pharaoh. Whereas he previously (8:28) had asked Moses to intercede for him, now he admits to sin: "I have sinned this time; the LORD is in the right, and I and my people are in the wrong" (9:27). Nevertheless, he once again reneges on his promise to let the Israelites go.

Pharaoh's next ploy is to put stipulations on who is to go: "Go, serve the LORD your God; but who is to go?" (10:8). After Moses responds that all go, men, women, and cattle, Pharaoh grants permission only to the men: "Look, you have some evil purpose in mind. No! Go, the men among you, and serve the LORD, for that is what you desire" (10:10–11). He apparently knows that if women, children, and cattle stay behind, the men are bound to return. Since we know that the request to go for a three days' journey is a trick, Pharaoh's stipulation is to the point. He proves himself to be a tough negotiator, and fortunately so, for otherwise the succession of plagues would lose its suspense. After the locusts descend on the land, he again confesses his sin (10:16). He is, it would seem, moving closer to a recognition of Yahweh not only as powerful but as righteous. After the ninth plague, the darkness, he makes a further concession: not only men but women and children may go. Only the flocks must remain behind (10:24). Like many a skillful bargainer he appears to give something without really giving anything. For the Israelites would still have to return to Egypt for their flocks. Obviously, this concession is not agreeable to Moses, who counters, again quite reasonably: "You must also let us have sacrifices and burnt offerings, that we may sacrifice to the LORD our God. Our cattle also must go with us" (10:25–26).

Not until the last and most terrible plague, the death of the Egyptian firstborn, does Pharaoh give in completely: "Rise up, go forth from among my people, both you and the people of Israel; and go, serve the LORD, as you have said. Take your flocks and your herds, as you have said, and be gone. . ." (12:31–32). This statement signals Pharaoh's capitulation to Yahweh. At the same time he asks for a blessing from Yahweh. "And bless me also" (12:32). This request is the final in a series of confessions by Pharaoh, and the series taken together describes the course of his acknowledgment of Yahweh as a god to whom worship is properly due. First he requests intercession, then he confesses his sin, and finally he asks for a blessing.

THE DENOUEMENT

Inasmuch as the purpose of the contest between Moses and Pharaoh has been to convince Pharaoh that Moses' God, Yahweh, is in fact lord of the land, it is achieved at this point, after the last plague. The story cannot end here, however. Whereas in *The Bacchae* Dionysus comes to Thebes with his followers already gathered into a worshiping community, Yahweh has not yet succeeded in making the Israelites a free and independent people. For this to come about the Israelites must escape from Egypt, and Pharaoh, who has all along prevented the coming together of Yahweh's community, must be destroyed. Both of these events have been prefigured by the last plague, the death of the Egyptian firstborn, as well as by Moses' murder of the Egyptian man and subsequent flight to Midian. As the Israelites exit, Yahweh lays his trap:

Then the LORD said to Moses, "Tell the people of Israel to turn back and encamp in front of Pihahiroth, between Migdol and the sea, in front of Baalzephon. . . . For Pharaoh will say of the people of Israel, 'They are entangled in the land; the wilderness has shut them in.' And I will harden Pharaoh's heart, and he will pursue them and I will get glory over Pharaoh and all his host; and the Egyptians shall know that I am the LORD." (14:1–4)

Sure enough, Pharaoh falls into the trap and he and his army perish. As a result Yahweh triumphs over the Egyptians before the very eyes of the Hebrews, and Moses' leadership is vindicated: "And Israel saw the great work which the LORD did against the Egyptians, and the people feared the LORD; and they believed in the LORD and in his servant Moses" (14:31).

The story ends with the now intact community singing Yahweh's praises: "I will sing to the LORD, for he has triumphed gloriously; the horse and his rider he has thrown into the sea" (15:1).

Returning now to the definition of comedy as a story in which the hero is finally incorporated into the society to which he properly belongs, we recognize that Exodus 1–15 is a comedy. It has two heroes. The visible, immediate hero is Moses. The story begins with his estrangement from his kinsmen at birth and moves through his return to his people and final acceptance by them as leader. The invisible, ultimate hero is Yahweh. The story begins with estrangement, both physical (Yahweh is in Midian and his people in Egypt) and social/religious (Pharaoh is their king whereas Yahweh should be), and ends with reunion. The means by which the two heroes are integrated with their proper societies is the agon, or contest, between Moses and Pharaoh. As often in comedy at its best, this integration represents the establishment of a new community, a socially free and morally just one, which replaces an old, unjust one. As also often in comedy, the birth of the new society is marked by some festive celebration which ends the story or play (Exod. 15).

In most comedies there is a blocking agent, an *alazon*, an impostor, who obstructs the hero's path to the land of the free and home of the brave. Pharaoh, of course, is this agent. He must either be incorporated into the new society or cast out from it, in which case he becomes a *pharmakos*, or scapegoat. Because comedy as a genre tends toward the happiest possible ending, in many comedies the blocking agent is incorporated into the new society. Such is not the case in Exodus, where Pharaoh and his army are destroyed. Exodus is like most comedies, however, in that the force which brings about the overthrow of the *alazon* comes from beyond the human world, from Fate, or Chance, or the gods.

The Bacchae ends very differently from Exodus 1–15. Euripides focuses our attention, not on the triumphant Dionysus and his followers, but on Pentheus' family, so that he, not Dionysus, becomes the hero of the play, that is, the person from whose point of view we primarily view and understand the action. In so doing Euripides makes *The Bacchae* into a tragedy, a work in which the hero is alienated from the society to which he properly belongs: instead of being king over Thebes Pentheus has been cruelly murdered. (One might compare how Exodus would read if, after the death of Pharaoh, the narrative took us back to Egypt to view the catastrophe from the perspective of Pharaoh's bereft family.) In one of the greatest and most excruciating recognition scenes in all of tragedy, we witness Pentheus' mother, Agave, his murderer, return to Thebes thinking the head she waves so triumphantly in the air is a wild lion, and then watch Cadmus, her father, gradually bring her out from under the god's spell to the recognition that it is her son:

C. First raise your eyes to the heavens.
A.   There.
     But why?
C.   Does it look the same as it did before?
     Or has it changed?

A.   It seems—somehow—clearer,
brighter than it was before.

C.   Do you still feel
the same flurry inside you?

A.   The same—flurry?
No, I feel—somehow—calmer. I feel as though—
my mind were somehow—changing.

C.   Can you still hear me?
Can you answer clearly?

A.   No. I have forgotten
what we were saying, Father.

C.   Who was your husband?

A. Echion—a man, they said, born of the dragon seed.

C. What was the name of the child you bore your husband?

A. Pentheus.

C.   And whose head do you hold in your hands?

A. A lion's head—or so the hunters told me.

C. Look directly at it. Just a quick glance.

A. What is it? What am I holding in my hands?

C. Look more closely still. Study it carefully.

A. No! O gods, I see the greatest grief there is.

C. Does it look like a lion now?

A.   No, no. It is—
Pentheus' head—I hold—   (lines 1264–84)

The story ends with Cadmus and Agave departing the stage cursed by
Dionysus to live in exile.

AMBIGUITY, AMBIVALENCE, AND IRONY

The ending of *The Bacchae* profoundly influences our attitude
toward the characters in the play. Pentheus has been presented to us
as a man ignorant of what it is most important to know: one's place
in the universe. Because of his ignorance he has acted most foolishly.
Yet the ending forces us to see that he has a good side also: after all,
he is trying to defend his kingdom against what he perceives, not
entirely without justification, as a moral license that will shatter his
state. In other words, Pentheus is somewhat good, somewhat evil.
He is ambiguous, and our reaction to him is, therefore, ambivalent.

The same ambivalence applies to Dionysus. He is a god, a god
wronged, slandered. Yet, as we watch Agave's cruel enlightenment,
we cannot help but wonder whether any god who perpetrates such
suffering deserves the name of god. Cadmus puts to Dionysus the
pointed question: should a god be so ruled by the all too human
emotion of vengeance? Dionysus has no good answer.

Turning from these two principal dramatis personae, we find that
moral ambiguity characterizes every player and every scene in this
tragedy. Cadmus and Teiresias, the blind seer, supposedly represent
the wisdom of old age, yet they appear early in the play pathetically

and ridiculously dressed in Dionysiac livery, and expound only commonplace and self-justifying wisdom. Or take the chorus. These worshipers of the god are nevertheless extraordinarily bloodthirsty throughout, and positively overcome with joy when Pentheus is slain.

As a result of these ambiguities, ironies abound in the play. Pentheus is blind to Dionysus' true status as a god, yet he sees Dionysus' capacity for promoting social disruption and personal suffering. Agave sees the god, yet is blind to her son. Dionysus, too, sees, yet is blind in the sense of being unfeeling toward human suffering. The less Pentheus dresses like Dionysus, the more he acts as any sane king might act in the face of social disorder; the more he dresses like Dionysus, a god, with curls and long skirts, the more demonically he behaves. In fact, Euripides sets up a symbolic equation in the play: put on the god's livery, take off human wisdom. And when we remember that Dionysian worship involved the sacrifice of an animal considered by the community to be a substitute for Dionysus himself, another and greater irony appears: Pentheus dies as a scapegoat and, therefore, as a surrogate for the very god he rejects. And the greatest irony of all is that this play, this terrible indictment of Dionysus was presented in none other than the theater of Dionysus. The capacity of *The Bacchae* to absorb irony seems infinite, and with each additional irony the play becomes greater. No wonder its status as one of the world's literary masterpieces!

Returning now to Exodus, we can see why it is so crucial that we be given no cause for sympathizing with Pharaoh. Since Exodus 1–15 casts out its blocking agent, for the story to work we must be thoroughly convinced that his exclusion is right and just. Even a little sympathy for Pharaoh would qualify the spontaneity with which we join with Moses in singing Yahweh's praises. What happens when the audience has reason to sympathize with an exorcised *alazon* can be seen in Shakespeare's *Merchant of Venice*. Especially when Shylock is played by a strong actor, the audience is generally confused—is this drama the tragedy of Shylock or the comedy of the lovers? It is a measure of the greatness of Shakespeare that his play seems to gain in stature from this ambiguity. Such ambiguity in Exodus 1–15 would be utterly disastrous, especially since the new society that it creates is clearly not only the socially proper society but the morally just one. Ambiguity obfuscates moral clarity. By and large, Exodus 1–15 successfully keeps our sympathy entirely with Moses.

Nor can Exodus tolerate irony. But it does not quite keep us from thinking ironic thoughts. For example, it is ironic that the righteous

Yahweh himself has to harden the tyrannical Pharaoh's heart to keep the series of plagues going. The situation is reminiscent of Dionysus having to cast a spell on Pentheus to get him to dress in woman's clothes. Neither situation redounds to the god's credit. Or an even more disturbing example. Pharaoh is a scapegoat, whose death makes possible Exodus' new society. Usually a scapegoat is considered to be a surrogate for the community itself, so like that community that it can act as a substitute for it. Such thoughts suggest that perhaps the Israelites and the Egyptians were not so very different after all. And one final example. Is it really possible for a just society to arise out of the wholesale slaughter of its opponents? Unlike the irony in *The Bacchae* such thoughts detract from Exodus 1–15, becloud its issues, and qualify its mood. In other words, whereas the effectiveness of *The Bacchae* depends upon its capacity to absorb ambiguity and irony, the effectiveness of Exodus 1–15 depends upon its ability to exclude them.

PRACTICE FOR LIVING

In Chapter I we suggested that one of the values of literature is the practice it gives us in living. Following up that idea we can ask what feelings the reader has while reading Exodus 1–15 and *The Bacchae*, and what attitudes about life follow from these feelings. Let us take Exodus 1–15 first. We can diagram the plot structure and the emotional valences of the reader as follows:

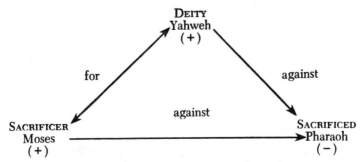

Yahweh is for Moses and against Pharaoh, and supplies Moses with the power to destroy Pharaoh. Moses and Yahweh are presented to us as all good (+) and Pharaoh as all evil (−). Whether the reader identifies with Moses, as he will naturally do in the course of reading the story, or with Pharaoh, or surveys the whole, he will experience essentially childlike emotions (I love my side, I hate my enemy) and learn essentially childlike lessons (I am good, my enemy is bad, god is on my side, god is not on my side).

The plot structure of *The Bacchae* is identical to that of Exodus, yet the emotional valences the reader experiences are entirely different:

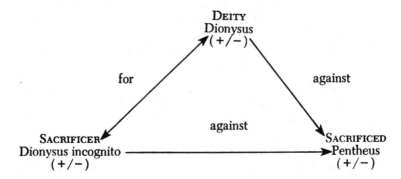

Whether the reader identifies with Pentheus, as he is led naturally to do, or with Dionysus and the chorus, or surveys the whole, he experiences essentially adult emotions (ambivalence toward self, others, and the gods) and learns essentially adult lessons (I am good and bad; my enemy is partly good, partly bad, as are the gods). To sum up, then, in terms of certain rather fundamental human values (the complexity of the adult world over against the simplicity of the child's), it is preferable to practice living by reading *The Bacchae* than by reading Exodus 1–15.

It is rather interesting to realize how many plots in the Old Testament are similar to that of Exodus 1–15. Take the following as illustrations:

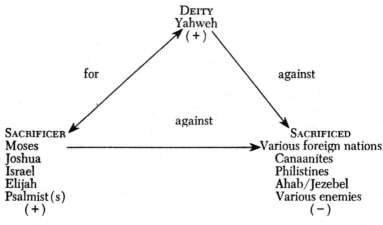

Exceptions exist, of course, but they remain exceptional, not only because they do not fit the rule but because they tend to be the greatest pieces of literature in the Old Testament: the stories of Saul, David, Jonah, Job. On the other hand, it is startling to realize how much of Greek literature is characterized by the same ambiguity and irony we find in *The Bacchae*: the *Iliad* (note, in contrast to Exodus' treatment of Pharaoh, the scene depicting Hector's wife and children), virtually all of Greek tragedy, Plato's *Republic*, Aristotle, Thucydides, and most of Aristophanes. To venture, then, into an old and heated debate, can we not say that reading Greek literature as a whole is better practice for adult living than reading Hebrew literature as a whole?

I would like to end this chapter by a brief excursion into the New Testament. The characterization and plot of the Gospel of Mark are, except at one vital point, virtually identical to *The Bacchae*. The deity is the Lord, Jesus is the deity incognito, who must prove his claim to godhood against the unbelievers, the Jews and Romans. The crucial difference is, of course, that instead of Jesus killing the Jews and Romans, they kill him. So we have the diagram:

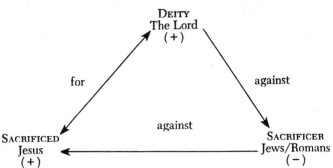

The relationships between the characters are the same as in *The Bacchae* (deity is for his incognito and against the unbelievers) but the positions of sacrificed and sacrificer are reversed. Most interesting to me, however, is that Mark is like Exodus in being unable to admit irony, so that the emotional valences of the reader are as in Exodus 1–15. The Jews and Romans are wholly in the wrong and Jesus wholly in the right. An attempt even partially to justify the Jews and Romans or raise ethical questions of Jesus' actions ruins the intended effect of the story.

Since Jesus really is a god, it is not surprising that the above diagram only describes the anticlimax of Mark. Once Jesus has been raised, and thereby, comedy snatched from the gaping jaws of tragedy, the diagram must be revised as follows, with the addendum that the sacrifice of the unbelievers is projected into the future:

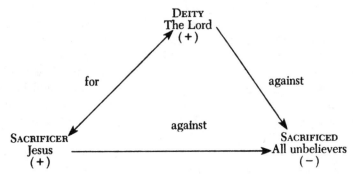

In other words, the situation is exactly the same as in Exodus 1–15. The only way the unbelievers (whether Jew or Gentile) can avoid being sacrificed is by admitting their guilt in killing the disguised deity and thereby changing allegiances, which is exactly what the early Christian preachers urged them to do, according to Acts. My main point is that, in spite of the difference between Exodus 1–15 and Mark in terms of plot, Mark teaches the same childlike emotional lessons as Exodus. As literature *The Bacchae* is as superior to both of them as the adult world is superior to the child's.

III

The Book of Job[1]

Abraham Lincoln said that the United States was "one nation, indivisible." Since the states were not one in fact, it is clear that their unity was more of a premise from which he worked, a premise that determined, in turn, how he handled the divided states in practice. As was stressed in Chapter I literary critics generally make a similar assumption about literary texts. No matter how complicated the history of a text's composition, once the process of interpretation begins, it is taken as if it were a unified whole. Consequently, the practice of literary criticism will inevitably involve a demonstration that the text is indeed a unified whole (by means of a careful, painstaking interrelating of its parts), together with comments about how this unity is achieved. The circular character of the critic's task could hardly be more apparent. One assumes that a text is a whole and then proceeds to show that indeed it is a whole. Not that it gives much comfort, but it is hard to see that Lincoln operated any differently.

With many literary works a demonstration of unity is easily accomplished: its parts nicely harmonize and add up to a symphonic whole that has a straightforward, unambiguous theme. With other works, however, the situation is similar to the one that faced Lincoln. Try to force unity and you create tension, disharmony, ambiguity, and the like. The causes of these dissonances are legion. Perhaps a dramatis persona acts in one part in ignorance of what transpires in another part. Or possibly a metaphor is used in one place in a way that seems incompatible with its use elsewhere. Or maybe a character is inexplicably dropped from the narrative, or a new one inserted seemingly from nowhere. But whatever the cause the effect is nearly always some form of irony.

1. Portions of this chapter originally appeared in *Soundings, An Interdisciplinary Journal*, vol. 56 (1973), 446–69, and are reprinted with the permission of the publisher.

The interpretation of Job presented in this chapter is a result of taking the premise of unity with utmost seriousness. I take the book in its received form and continually push one question: what does this part of the text mean when it is read in light of all the other parts? The answer in virtually every case is that it has an ironic, not a straightforward, meaning. I conclude in the end that irony pervades the entire book and provides the decisive key to understanding its complicated theme.

THE PROSE STORY

The prose story is possibly best labeled a didactic folk tale. The conventions of this genre are everywhere apparent: this is a "once upon a time" tale; the characters are not realistically drawn but are defined by stereotyped formulas; the plot is conventional, the story of a man who, though supreme among men, is subjected to terrible trials, through which he emerges triumphant only by the supreme exercise of his greatness. Moreover, the repetition of set formulas, the economy of language, and the charm are all characteristics of the style of folk tales.

The first five verses of chapter 1 introduce us to the hero. Job is presented to us as the paragon of humanity: he was "blameless and upright, one who feared God and shunned evil" (v. 1).[2] The word translated "blameless" is the Hebrew tām, which means whole, complete, integral, as, say, the circle is whole, complete, integral; the word translated "upright" is the Hebrew yāšār, which means, not standing up as opposed to lying down, but straight as opposed to crooked. In verse 1, then, we are informed that Job is perfect as the circle and the straight line are perfect. The idea of perfection is further emphasized by the arithmetic of his possessions. He has seven (a perfect number) sons and three (another perfect number) daughters. He has seven thousand sheep, three thousand camels, and five (a third perfect number) hundred yoke of oxen and five hundred she-asses. Then, in order to illustrate Job's perfection, the story gives us an example of his perfect piety. His sons were in the habit of celebrating a round of feast days. So great was his piety that early in the morning on the day following the seven-day round he would ritually purify them by sacrifice, just in case they had sinned during their festivities.

2. All translations in this chapter, unless otherwise noted, are from *Job* (Anchor Bible), translated and edited by Marvin H. Pope (New York: Doubleday, 1965). Copyright © 1965 by Doubleday & Company, Inc. Used by permission of the publisher.

The scene now switches to heaven and we meet the two other principal characters in this story. The sons of God periodically gathered around God, their king, for meetings of the heavenly council. One of their number was "the Satan." This term designates an office, like our Attorney General, and not a person (hence, "the Satan," not "Satan"). His job is to insure that God is duly and sincerely worshiped and to prosecute the negligent. He is not the enemy of man that the Devil of Christian theology is, his task being not to tempt man to evil but to spot evil men. Likewise the Satan is not the enemy of God; rather he is God's servant. But in this case it does seem that a kind of rivalry has sprung up between them. God's pride is at stake. He wishes to be loved and respected for who he is, not just because he is the mightiest being in the universe. The Satan doubts that any man loves God for God's sake; he thinks men will lick any hand that feeds them.

But God believes he has found himself an ace of a man, the ace of trumps. So at this gathering of the royal council he says to the Satan, in essence, "Here is a man, Job, who worships me for my own sake." But the Satan is not God's chief prosecutor for nothing; he is as clever as his Christian counterpart, and is ready with an answer (vv. 9–11). He says, in effect, "How can you claim that Job worships you for nothing when you have given him such bounty? To make it a fair test of his loyalty you will have to withhold your rewards. If you do, may I be damned if he doesn't curse you to your face." In ancient Israel a curse was not an expletive but an effective word that necessarily set in motion a series of actions. The Satan's curse forces God's hand. He must proceed to test Job to see if the Satan will, in fact, be damned by some nameless catastrophe. If Job does curse God, the Satan is freed from the workings of the curse; if he doesn't, the curse will fulfill itself.[3] What Job says after the test is the hinge of the dramatic action. Then God sends forth the Satan to begin the test (v. 12).

The Satan reduces Job's possessions to nothing, and his family to almost nothing (vv. 13–19), leaving his wife, for whom, it seems, he has a purpose. And now we wait to hear what Job will say. He tears his clothes, shaves his head (both signs of mourning), and blesses God:

> Naked I came from my mother's womb
> And naked shall I return there.

3. I am indebted for this interpretation to Edwin M. Good, "Job and the Literary Task," *Soundings*, vol. 56 (1973), 474–76.

Yahweh gave, Yahweh took away.
Blessed be Yahweh's name. (v. 21)

God is proved right, but this turns out to be only round one. When the heavenly council reconvenes, God confronts the Satan with his apparent victory (2:3), only to discover that the Satan is not bested so easily. He thinks that the test has been superficial, that so long as a man does not suffer physical pain he can take most anything, and so proposes that he be allowed to attack Job's own flesh (vv. 4–5). God accepts the new conditions but imposes one restraint—the Satan must not kill Job, which, of course, would end the story without settling the issue (v. 6). The Satan carries out the proposed measures (v. 7), and again Job blesses God (v. 10), in spite of the assistance the Satan gets from Job's wife (v. 9).

At this point it would seem that the story is over. We expect to be returned to heaven and listen to God claim his victory. But instead we hear that three friends of Job have come to console him (vv. 11–13). Nothing so far has hinted that anything like this would happen. It breaks the close construction of the plot and so prepares for some intensification of the drama.

THE DIALOGUES

Chapter 3
After seven days Job curses his birth day: "Damn the day I was born" (3:3). The main question we need to ask is this: How does his doing so affect the plot? The outcome of the story depends on whether Job curses or blesses God. In response to two rounds of testing Job has blessed God. And now, without an intervening third round, he . . . does what? In my opinion he curses God. To be sure, he does this indirectly. His curse of his birth day is in effect a curse of all days. That is, he curses all creation by cursing what is for him its most significant part—the day of his birth—and to curse the creation is by implication to curse the creator.

Let's look at one part of his curse, verse 8, "Let the Sea-cursers damn it,/Those skilled to stir Leviathan." The Sea (Hebrew *yām*) and Leviathan are two names of the sea monster who is a personification of chaos and who fought against God at the time of creation. After God's victory he secured the land (because in the Hebrew conception the sea lies not only to the side of the land but under it) by anchoring it onto the back of the slain monster by means of pillars. But it turns out that the monster is not dead once and for all; she is capable of reviving herself. When she begins to flex her back muscles, she threatens—because the earth's pillars are resting on her—to throw creation back into chaos. Thus the creation, once established, is not forever secure; it must ever be secured. Job's wish, then, is that the practitioners of black magic may succeed in rousing the monster so that she can pitch his day, and, metaphorically, all creation back into chaos. This amounts to a preference of chaos over creation, a preference that can only be taken as an implied curse on the creator.

If this interpretation of chapter 3 is correct, then the Satan's prediction of what Job would do when tested is now in the process of being fulfilled. The movement of the plot has been reversed. It looks, at this point at least, as if the Satan may be freed from his curse. And on the basis of the allegiances set up in the folk tale this reversal should be upsetting to us the readers. Within the conventions of the folk tale we are led naturally to sympathize with the hero. Thus we want Job to bless God. So, when Job curses God in chapter 3 we should withdraw our sympathy from him. Yet what we should do we do not do. If anything, our identification with him increases in the course of chapter 3. Our refusal to abandon Job is explained, I think, by the fact that as we go from the folk tale to chapter 3 we go from a fairy tale-like world into the real world. Job so gives voice to our own fears, doubts, and frustrations that we cannot help but sympathize with him. And identification with Job means approval of his cursing God. Thus we become one of the Satan's party without our quite knowing what has happened. What began as a test of Job's loyalty to God has turned into a test of God's loyalty to Job. As will become increasingly clear as Job and the friends debate, God is the one now on trial.

Chapters 4 and 5

After Job's curse of his birth day the first of the friends, Eliphaz, speaks. Through the first eleven verses his argument is easy enough to follow: Job, you yourself have comforted people when calamity has befallen them (vv. 3–4), so now, when calamity befalls you, you should not panic but remember your own advice (v. 5), which is that any religious man should remember in the midst of distress that his religion is his hope (v. 6). Regardless of how bad things get, no righteous man ever perishes; rather it is only the wicked who perish (vv. 7–11).

But when we come to verses 12–21, problems begin to arise. In a trance one night the true relationship between God and man was vouchsafed to Eliphaz (vv. 12–16). God alone is truly just and pure

(v. 17). Even the angels, who are not made from such perishable stuff as dust, are guilty before him (v. 18). How much more guilty then are men, who are made of clay. While this argument is consistent enough when taken alone, it is somewhat puzzling to know how to relate it to the first eleven verses. Here Eliphaz says that all men are impure in God's eyes, whereas there he spoke of the innocent and the righteous. Here he says that all men perish, whereas there he claimed that only the wicked perish. This puzzle can possibly be unscrambled in the following way. In verses 12–21 Eliphaz is trying to explain to Job why he, though an essentially righteous man, cannot escape *some* suffering. All men are less than wholly righteous in God's sight and therefore are destined for a certain amount of correctional punishment. Crucial in Eliphaz' eyes is a man's response to this discipline. If he plays the fool by chafing at God's correction, then calamity will befall him (5:1–5). But if he follows Eliphaz' advice and profits by God's chastening (5:8), then he will be fortunate in the end (5:17), and Eliphaz will have been right in his claim, made in 4:1–11, that their piety is the hope of the righteous.

On the basis of the content of his speech, Eliphaz deserves some real sympathy from the reader. He seems sincerely convinced of Job's piety, accounting for Job's misfortune by appealing to a revealed doctrine of the inherent sinfulness of mankind, thereby implicating Job in sin not because he is an evil man but because he is human. And while he does openly rebuke Job's rash speech in chapter 3, we should remember that almost anyone would judge Job's speech rash. Thus Eliphaz comes across for the most part as one understandably alarmed at his friend's heresy and anxious to correct it on the basis of convictions forged out of his own religious experience. Furthermore, given the folk tale, he has Job's situation sized up rather well. In chapters 1–2 we learned that Job really is pious in God's eyes, and that his piety is being tested.

Yet we cannot help being somewhat offended at his rather pompous attitude toward himself: although he comes as a comforter, he is terribly self-righteous, appealing to a private vision to authenticate his theology and making himself in 5:8 the exemplar of the wise response to chastisement. And, further, his descriptions of the wicked in 4:8–11 and the fool in 5:2–5 come perilously close to being descriptions of Job's own plight, especially when we remember, after reading his assertion in 4:9 that the wicked perish by the breath of God, that Job's sons died in a great wind. Thus we have good reasons for suspecting that Eliphaz' positive attitude toward Job may be merely a thin epidermis concealing a deep hostility underneath.

Chapters 6 and 7

In his answer to Eliphaz, Job justifies his rash speech in chapter 3; he lays out his case against God. But his indictment does not proceed logically, from premises to conclusions; it consists, rather, of a rambling repetition of several fundamental themes. The impression that the two chapters as a whole make is that of an impromptu, impassioned, rhetorically overstated plea in his own defense.

To begin with he says that God is attacking him. He uses, for the most part, military imagery to describe God's assaults. He thinks that God is using the sickness-causing demons as poison arrows and says that God is shooting them at him, so that his life is soaking up their venom (6:4). Of course, no disagreement exists between Job and Eliphaz on this point. But whereas Eliphaz thinks that God's attacks are justified, Job thinks that they are wholly unwarranted.

His fundamental argument, both here and in the chapters that follow, is that he is essentially innocent: "I have not denied the Holy One's words" (6:10c). This does not mean that he thinks himself sinless; rather it means that he thinks his punishment is totally out of proportion to his crimes. He thinks that God should be able to forgive him:

> Why not pardon my fault,
> Forgive my iniquity? (7:21)

After all, he is not the Sea or the Dragon (7:12). That God should attack them is wholly understandable, for they are bent on precipitating a return to chaos. But he is no enemy of God, and, furthermore, is utterly helpless even to defend himself (6:11–13). Therefore God's assaults on him are unjustified. He makes this point in one of the most brilliant parodies in biblical literature. The author of Psalm 8 believes that God's special attention to man is wholly out of proportion with man's size and status and so is a sign of God's grace:

> When I look at your heavens, the work of your hands,
> At the moon and the stars that you have made,
> What is man that you consider him,
> Or mankind that you visit them?
> Yet you have made him only a little lower than the gods,
> And crowned him with glory and honor. (my translation)

Job agrees that man is very small and very helpless, and so he cannot understand why God persecutes him so:

> I will not live forever.
> Hold off, for my days are a breath.
> Why do you rear man at all,
> Or pay any mind to him?

> Inspect him every morning,
> And test him every moment? (7:16–18)

Because Job believes that God is attacking him and that this attack is unjustified, he concludes that God is guilty of foul play. And he thinks that he is not so undiscriminating that he cannot see that it is foul play. He draws a parallel with domestic animals. Just as the ass does not complain when he is well fed, but only when he is hungry, so Job complains only because he thinks God is serving him flat, tasteless food (6:5–7). Because God has made life so miserable for him, in a bitter parody of the petitionary language of the psalms he wishes that God would grant him his entreaty—kill him and so release him from so much pain:

> O that my entreaty might be granted,
> That God might reward my hope:
> That it please God to crush me,
> Loose his hand and snip me.
> That would even be my comfort. (6:8–10a)

Then at the conclusion of this speech he again startles us by his reversal of typical Hebrew values. He asks for forgiveness:

> Why not pardon my fault,
> Forgive my iniquity? (7:21a)

For the ordinary man forgiveness means restoration to health and happiness. But Job believes that God is keeping him alive only to persecute him. Thus forgiveness would mean for him that God would permit him to die, so that he would no longer be around when God came to hound him

> That I might now lie in the dust,
> And you seek me but I would not be. (7:21b)

Because of his great pain and because of his powerful rhetoric Job has no difficulty in gaining our sympathy. In fact, it is likely that most readers tend to go too far in their identification with him. It should be remembered that his attack on God is truly virulent, and, on the basis of the folk tale, unjustifiably so. We may think that God is somewhat thick-skinned in testing Job, but we should remember that the test is a necessary consequence of the Satan's self-curse, and, therefore, not something for which God is morally responsible. Moreover, God has been motivated by the desire to answer a profound religious question, "Does man worship God for what he can get out of it?" In no way is God the demonic monomaniac that Job pictures him as being.

Chapter 8

Bildad, unlike the more deferential Eliphaz, is hard-hitting:

You, Job, are full of hot air. God does not pervert justice. Therefore, if your sons sinned, then they got what they deserved. As for you, if you will turn to God, he will heal you, if you are truly upright, as you say you are, and you will have a glorious future. (paraphrase of 8:2–7)

But, having said this, Bildad seems to realize that his logic is having no effect on Job, because Job will not grant the premise from which his conclusions follow—that God does not pervert justice. So he tries to convince Job of the validity of his reasoning by appealing to authority. He needs, however, a higher authority than himself and his two friends, for Eliphaz has already appealed to whatever authority they might have without result (cf. 5:27). So he appeals to the authority of the forefathers (vv. 8–9). If Job would only consult them, they would tell him that God is just.

Chapter 9

Job's speech in chapter 9 shows a definite logical progression. He begins, "Indeed, I know that this is so: how can a man be ṣādēq before God?" (my translation). Curiously, Job is ignoring Bildad and still responding to Eliphaz, for the rhetorical question asked by Eliphaz' apparition in 4:17 was, "Can a man be ṣādēq before God?" (my translation). As the following verses indicate, the expected answer is no. Here in chapter 9 Job seems to agree—but the agreement is only apparent. Actually, Job and Eliphaz are using the Hebrew root ṣdq in two different senses. Eliphaz is using it in its religious sense of "being righteous." He thinks that man cannot be righteous before God because of his inferior ontological status. Job is using the root in its juridical sense of "being innocent." No man, Job believes, could get a verdict of innocent in a suit against God because God is too clever and too powerful:

> If he [a man] wished to go to court with him [God],
> He could not answer him one in a thousand questions.
> He is the clever and powerful one,
> Who could go against him and come out in one piece?
> (vv. 3–4, my translation)

Much of the remainder of the chapter is a rhetorical defense of Job's thesis. He argues from the greater to the lesser. In verses 5–13 he pictures God as so powerful and so inaccessible that even the other gods are helpless before him. How much less, then, could he, a mere mortal, match words with him in court (vv. 14–20). Then in

41

verse 33 he introduces an idea that is to play a crucial role in the chapters that follow: the idea of a third party. Here the function of this party is to guarantee a fair trial:

> He is not, like me, a man whom I could challenge,
> "Let us go to court together."
> Would there were an umpire between us
> To lay his hand on us both. (vv. 32–33)

In chapters 6–7 Job was trying by and large to justify himself to the friends, but they, on the evidence of Bildad's speech, proved unsympathetic. So at the beginning of chapter 9 he conceives of presenting his case before God, but quickly realizes the folly of this plan, since he and God are not peers. Consequently, at the end of chapter 9 he hopes for a disinterested party who could insure a fair trial.

Chapter 11

Now we meet the third of the trio of friends, Zophar. Eliphaz appealed to whatever authority the friends themselves might have, Bildad to the authority of past generations. Zophar appeals to nothing less than the nature of God himself. His is the ploy surely most often used by "comforters": the ways of God are beyond human understanding; therefore we must not accuse him of wrongdoing when things happen that we do not comprehend. But Zophar is no longer really trying to comfort. He has become so incensed at Job's persistence in his heresy that he wants Job's ignorance exposed; and who can do that better than God himself?

> You say, "My doctrine is pure."
> You are clean in your own eyes.
> But would that God might speak,
> Might open his lips against you;
> He would tell you what is hidden. (vv. 4–6a)

We have seen that Job easily gains our sympathy. By now it is clear that the friends just as easily manage to antagonize us. Their self-righteousness and their condescension toward Job are highly irritating. Yet their theology seems generally sound, and in fact, is corroborated by the folk tale, which demonstrates that no righteous man perishes in the end (Eliphaz' claim), that God does not distort justice (Bildad's claim), and that some things are indeed beyond man's ken (Zophar's claim). Thus, we are likely somewhat torn in our affections at this point in the book. We want to sympathize with Job, and yet are disturbed by the rashness of his remarks about God; we want to repudiate the friends and yet have to concede that their theology is more appropriate to the God of the folk tale than is Job's.

Chapter 12

In verses 12–25 of chapter 12 Job employs a technique he has used before: a tongue-in-cheek agreement with the friends. In 9:2 he seemingly agreed with Eliphaz that a man could not be *ṣādēq* before God, only to show how great was his disagreement. Here he appears to agree with Zophar that God is wise (v. 13). But then he proceeds to describe God's wisdom as manifested in his creation, and it turns out not to be wisdom at all but the sheerest folly. When a wise man tears down, he does so with an eye to reconstruction. But God so thoroughly destroys that rebuilding is impossible: "If he tear down, there is no rebuilding" (v. 14a). If a wise man could control the weather, he would bring rain when needed and sun when needed. But God either brings so much rain that all is flooded, or he makes the sun shine until all is scorched:

> If he withholds the waters, there is drought;
> Or lets them go, they engulf the earth. (v. 15)

And the list goes on. Clearly, in Job's opinion, God is not so wise.

Chapter 12 shows unmistakably that what began in the folk tale as a test of Job has become a test of God. Right from the start, of course, Job has made it clear that he does not consider his case unique. He has all along considered the question of God's faithfulness to him an aspect of the larger question of God's faithfulness to mankind. But in this chapter he goes beyond the problem of God's relation to mankind and charges him with mismanaging the universe as a whole.

The Second and Third Cycles: The Friends

The speeches of the friends in the second and third cycles become increasingly stereotyped: they are more explicit in their accusations that Job is a sinner, more vivid in their descriptions of the punishment awaiting the wicked, and more strident in their defense of God. In fact, now that God is also on trial, the friends can appropriately be thought of as God's self-appointed attorneys. Eliphaz' third speech, chapter 22, is the only one that I will consider here, for it represents the friends' only attempt to develop a solid argument against Job. Eliphaz begins:

> Can a man benefit God,
> Even a sage man benefit him?

43

> What good to Shaddai if you are just?
> What gain if your conduct be perfect?   (vv. 2–3)

Isolated from their context these verses may seem to expound a theory of divine impassivity. But once they are placed in context it becomes clear that this is not Eliphaz' meaning. If it were, then it would follow that God pays no attention to righteousness or wickedness. Yet Eliphaz' actual conclusion from verses 2–3 is that God punishes Job not for righteousness but for wickedness:

> Is it for your piety he reproves you,
> Enters into judgment with you?
> Is not your wickedness great?
> Are not your iniquities endless?   (vv. 4–5)

What Eliphaz is doing, therefore, is not stating a doctrine of divine impassivity but a doctrine of divine impartiality. Job has said that God is punishing him without cause. Eliphaz is retorting that this cannot be the case, since God is not dependent on man for anything and so can have no ulterior motive. Eliphaz' point can be illustrated by contrasting his statement here with Job's argument in 7:20. There Job said that man can do God no harm; therefore, why should God be so afraid of him? Here Eliphaz counters that since it is also true that man can do God no favors, God cannot be bribed, and so must be an impartial judge.

The Second and Third Cycles: Job

Job in the second round of speeches further develops the legal imagery he has used from the beginning. In chapters 6–7 he set forth his case against God. In chapter 9 he conceived of a trial with God as a way of establishing his innocence, but realized that he could not get a fair trial. So he wished for an umpire to guarantee a fair trial. In chapter 12 he broadened his case against God to include his mismanagement of the cosmos. Now in chapter 16 he imagines God as continuing to press his attacks upon him, so that finally he lies on the ground dead. He asks the earth not to cover up his spilled blood:

> His archers ring me round.
> He stabs my vitals without pity,
> Pours out my guts on the ground.
> He rushes at me like a warrior.
> . . . .
> O earth, cover not my blood,
> That there be no tomb for my plaint.   (vv. 13–14, 18)

The images in verse 18 refer to the situation of blood redemption. If a man was killed unjustly, then his spilled blood was pictured as calling out for vengeance, and it was the task of the slain man's next of kin, his kinsman redeemer (Hebrew: *gō'ēl*), to avenge the murder by killing the murderer. But curiously, Job does not at this point follow the imagery through.

In the verses that follow he imagines himself not dead but alive and goes back to the imagery of a trial. It seems that he still holds out some hope for a fair trial, and in this connection returns to the idea of a third party, only now this party is not an umpire but a witness, a go-between, someone to intercede with God on his behalf. And what is more, Job now does not wish for such a figure but affirms that he does exist:

> Even now my witness is in heaven,
> My guarantor is on high,
> Interpreter of my thoughts to God,
> Toward whom my eye drips
> While he pleads for a man with God,
> As a fellow does for his friend. (vv. 19–21)

Such confidence is somewhat belied by the final verse of the chapter, however. If this witness is going to help him, it will have to be soon, for he will not be around much longer:

> For the few years pass,
> The way of no return I go. (v. 22)

In chapter 19 Job returns once again to a description of God's attack upon him. God is depicted as a villainous murderer, a gangster who has trapped Job in his net. Job realizes the trap and shouts "Murder!" but there is no one to rescue him (vv. 6–7).

Nevertheless, he is sure that, if only his case were engraved in rock for all time, then later, after his death, a redeemer would arise:

> O that my words were written,
> Were engraved in copper,
> With an iron stylus on lead,
> Carved in rock for all time.
> I know my vindicator [Hebrew: *gō'ēl*] lives,
> A guarantor upon the dust will stand. (vv. 23–25)

Job is here returning and completing the blood redemption motif he first broached in chapter 16. He has despaired of being vindicated before his death; his only hope for justice lies now not in a trial but in vengeance. He is sure that a kinsman redeemer will hear the cry of his spilled blood and will avenge him by murdering his murderer, God. He has turned Hebrew orthodoxy topsy-turvy. The typical Hebrew thought that if a human kinsman failed to secure vengeance for him, God could be counted on to do so. Job thinks that God is not only obstructing justice but committing injustice, so he appeals to one who will assume God's role and slay God.

But is there a being who could act as Job's avenger? It would seem, despite Job's positive expectation, that the only possible answer is no, for Job all along concedes that God is the superior being in the universe. Furthermore, when we realize that Job never so much as alludes to this figure again, it seems fair to conclude that he himself knows that such a figure is a pipe dream. Surely he would not so quickly abandon the idea of an avenger if he thought that there were any substance to it. In a sense, he comes to the idea of a *gōʾēl* not because he has believed in such a being all along but because this is where his legal imagery has led him. Blood vengeance is the last recourse to one who has sought justice but has been denied it in his lifetime.

After chapter 19 and before chapters 29–31 Job says nothing new. In his remaining speeches he returns to the problem of finding justice before he dies and to countering the arguments of the friends. Only chapter 28 is likely to excite our interest. Structurally, it is parallel to Chapter 12: in both Job takes up the problem of wisdom and in both he makes statements that seem to be in line with the opinions of Eliphaz, Bildad, and Zophar, but that in context can only be read as sarcastic in the extreme. Mankind, though technologically skillful, has not found wisdom (vv. 1–20). Not even in death can it be found (vv. 21–22). Only God has been able to locate it (vv. 23–27), and he has graciously communicated its essence to man:

> Behold, the fear of the Lord that is wisdom;
> To turn from evil is understanding.

This is precisely the wisdom Job has followed all his life (chapters 1–2) and where has it got him: the ash-heap. Some wisdom!

In chapters 29–31 Job makes his peroration. Chapter 29 is a wish for the good old days when God was Job's friend. Chapter 30 is a description of Job's present plight, now that God has become his enemy. And chapter 31 is an oath of clearance in the form of a series of self-imprecations: if I have done such and such an evil, then let such and such a calamity come upon me:

> If my steps have strayed from the way,
> Or my heart followed my eyes,
> Or spot stuck to my hands;
> May I sow and another eat,
> And my offspring be uprooted.   (vv. 7–8)

Job has pleaded with God to appear to hear his case, but God has not responded. He has stated his case, but now there is no judge or jury to pass judgment. But he has a way to force a verdict, and this is the way he takes in chapter 31: self-imprecation. Failure of the curses to fall upon Job's head is tantamount to acquittal. Fulfillment of the curses is tantamount to conviction. So Job forces God's hand. God now must act one way or the other—bring or not bring the curses upon Job, or, if he chooses not to let the case be decided in this fashion, he will have to appear and render judgment in person. As Job ends his oath of clearance with one more plea for God to answer, we reach the climax toward which all the previous action has been heading. Job has reached the limit of what he can do to secure justice for himself; it is now up to God to act:

> O that someone would listen to me!
> Behold my signature, let Shaddai answer me.
> Let my opponent write a document.
> I would wear it on my shoulder,
> I would bind it on like a crown.
> I would tell him the number of my steps;
> I would approach him like a prince. (vv. 35–37)

A moment's reflection will show that the only real option God has is to appear personally and speak to Job. Neither of the other two alternatives would satisfactorily resolve the tensions of the plot. Fulfillment of the curses would be unsatisfactory because God himself in the prologue proclaimed Job's innocence. On the other hand, restoration of Job, while sustaining his innocence, would leave unanswered all the accusations he has made against God. So God must put in a personal appearance. And when he does so, he will have to do more than explain to Job the wager between him and the Satan. Such an explanation, though upholding Job's innocence, would again not speak to the accusations against God's innocence. Consequently, God has facing him not only an admission of Job's innocence but also a demonstration of his own innocence. Such a demonstration would not only resolve the intellectual complexities of the book but the emotional ones involved in our responses to the friends and Job. It would show that the friends were right in their theology (God does not pervert justice) but wrong in their assumption that because Job is suffering he must be a sinner; it would show that Job's complaint against God was warranted on the basis of the evidence available to him, but unwarranted in the larger scheme of things.

ELIHU

We expect God himself and get—Elihu, surely one of the supreme anticlimaxes in all of literature. Elihu is an extraordinarily comical figure. He is a youthful, high-spirited, pompous, cock-sure reincarnation of the friends. It takes him an interminably long time to introduce himself, and when he gets to his point, he adds nothing to what the friends have already said. He believes with Eliphaz that Job's suffering is corrective punishment because of sins, and that if Job will confess his wrongdoing, he will be restored to health. Elihu provides comic relief from the heaviness and acrimony of the debates between Job and his comforters, and as such he is most welcome. He also serves to prepare us for God. How he functions in this regard cannot be fully understood until we have encountered Yahweh himself.

GOD'S SPEECHES FROM THE STORM

God appears at this point and delivers two speeches. In these speeches God tries to convince Job and us of his innocence, that is, of the fact that he is a wise and just ruler of his world. He wants us to know that Job has been condemning him so that he, Job, might be justified (cf. 40:8). It is, however, clear that, when his speeches are placed within the context of what has preceded them, he fails utterly. Specifically, when what he does and says is considered in relation to what Job predicts he would do and say if he were to appear, it becomes apparent that his speeches are ironic at his own expense: they have an effect on Job and on us exactly opposite to the effect he desires. For example, Job says in 9:16-17:

> If I summoned and he answered,
> I do not believe he would heed me.
> He would crush with a tempest [Hebrew: $\check{s}^{e\prime}\bar{a}r\bar{a}h$].
> And multiply my wounds without cause.

Job is claiming that God would not come to listen patiently to Job's charges; he would come in a tornado, toss Job about, and scare him out of his wits.

And this is just what God does: he arrives in a whirlwind:

> Then Yahweh answered Job
> From out of the storm [Hebrew: $\check{s}^{e\prime}\bar{a}r\bar{a}h$].   (38:1)

Or, again, Job says in 9:2-4:

> Indeed, I know that this is so:
> How can a man be innocent before God?
> If he wished to go to court with him,
> He could not answer him one in a thousand questions.
> He is the clever and powerful one,
> Who could go against him and come out in one piece?
>   (my translation)

A mere mortal could not possibly win in a case against God, because God, as a skillful cross-examiner, would ask the man questions that he would be unable to answer. And this is precisely what God does to Job:

> Who is this that denies Providence
> With words void of knowledge?
> Gird your loins like a hero,
> I will ask you, and you tell me.
> Where were you when I founded the earth?
> Tell me, if you know so much.
> Who drafted its dimensions? Do you know?
> Who stretched the line over it?
> On what are its sockets sunk,
> Who laid its cornerstone,
> While the morning stars sang together,
> And all the gods exulted? (38:2–7)

Of course, Job cannot answer these questions. One would have to be God himself to answer them. So what do they prove? That Job is not God? But that is hardly at issue. Job has never claimed to be God. Consider, for example, 9:32: "He is not, like me, a man whom I could challenge." So, again, what do these questions prove? That God is powerful and knowledgeable? But this too has never been at issue. Job has reiterated his recognition of this fact time and again. What we need to know is how these questions relate to the case Job has made on his own behalf (that he is innocent) and against God (that he uses his power and knowledge unjustly). The answer is that they do not relate at all. God does not quiz Job about his life for the purpose of determining whether he really was righteous. Neither does he speak of the use to which he puts his power and knowledge. Job was right, then, in his prediction that God would not be fair, and was well advised to wish for an umpire (9:33).

Thus God comes in a storm to appear to Job and to us as awesome; but because Job has already prophesied that he would come in a storm, he seems not awesome but blustery. God asks Job questions he cannot answer to show up his ignorance, so that we will think that Job does not know what he is talking about and that he, God, is the wise one; yet, because Job has said he would ask unanswerable questions, Job comes off as the wise one and God seems wise only in the sense of being evasively cunning. It is as if you were told before meeting a certain professor that he was immensely learned but inept at straight thinking, an ineptness he tried to cover up by a show of rhetoric, and upon meeting him found this description correct. In this case, when the professor displays his rhetoric, it will not convince you, as he hopes it will, that he is an intellectual giant; rather it will convince you that he is inflated with knowledge he does not know how to use. So God's rhetoric, because Job has armed us against it, convinces us that he is a charlatan god, one who has the power and skill of a god but is a fake at the truly divine task of governing with justice and love.

Much else that Job says, while not, strictly speaking, a prediction of what God would do, nevertheless forms a part of the background against which we should measure him. Foremost in this category is Job's characterization of God's power and wisdom (cf. 12:13–25). God is depicted as awesomely powerful, but destructively so; as frightfully clever, but lacking in common sense. It is with these images in mind that God's descriptions of Leviathan and Behemoth should be read. These two monsters bear the same relationship toward man that Job pictures God as bearing. The two most prominent features of Job's picture of God, his terrible power and his utter disdain for man, are the two most prominent features in God's description of Leviathan and Behemoth. Since Job describes God as stupidly and disdainfully powerful, it seems fair to conclude that they become in a way symbols of God. The logic is that two things (God and the monsters) equal to the same thing (power stupidly and disdainfully used) are equal to each other.

This conclusion seems to be corroborated by a study of 40:19a. It reads, "He [Behemoth] is a primordial production of God." That is, Behemoth was among the first things God made when he created the world. In Prov. 8:22 personified Wisdom says of herself, "God begat me as his primordial production" (my translation). Behemoth, as a companion to Leviathan, ultimately symbolizes the powers of chaos, whereas Wisdom is the most comprehensive symbol ever used by the Hebrews to stand for all that is orderly. Wisdom symbolizes a world where the moral law within and the natural law without are in harmony, a world that is open and responsive to the desires and values of mankind; Behemoth symbolizes a world of disharmony, a world impervious to and destructive of the desires and values of mankind. So to say that Wisdom is the first thing God made is to affirm that the world is ultimately orderly. To say that Behemoth is the first thing God made is to affirm that the world is ultimately chaotic. And this latter affirmation is made by none other than God himself.[4]

---

4. For an alternative interpretation of Behemoth and Leviathan see Good, "Job and the Literary Task," pp. 480–81.

Given this interpretation of Leviathan and Behemoth, we can understand the function of God's descriptions of the wild ass (39:5-8), the
buffalo (39:9-12), the ostrich (39:13-18), the horse (39:19-25), the
hawk (39·26), and the eagle (39:27-30). They are pint-sized Leviathans, and as such lesser symbols of God.[5] Thus when God describes
the buffalo's disdain for man he is actually describing his own disdain.
And when he pictures the ostrich's lack of wisdom he is depicting his
own:

> The ostrich's wings flap wildly,
> Though her pinions lack feathers.
> She lays her eggs on the ground,
> Lets them be warmed in the dust.
> Heedless that foot may crush them,
> Some beast trample upon them.
> Her young she harshly rejects,
> Caring not if her labor be vain.　(39:13-16)

So, while God catalogues the characteristics of these animals and
those of Leviathan and Behemoth in order to impress Job and us with
how small Job is and how great he himself is as their maker, because
they turn out to resemble God so closely as he has been described to
us by Job, we conclude that God is great in the same way they are
great: in terms of a blind force that makes more for chaos than for
an ordered creation.

We have seen how Job has been right about God. But at this point
a question naturally arises: does not Job himself admit that he was
wrong and so by his own mouth refute the interpretation of God's
speeches presented here?

> I know that you can do all things;
> No purpose of yours can be thwarted.
> . . . .
> I talked of things I did not know,
> Wonders beyond my ken.
> . . . .
> I had heard of you by hearsay,
> But now my own eyes have seen you;
> So I recant and repent
> In dust and ashes.　(42:2-6)

But Job, at the same time that he was predicting what God would
do were he to appear, also predicted what he would have to do:

> No god can withstand his wrath,
> Rahab's troops cringe beneath him.

5. For an alternative interpretation of these animals see William Whedbee, "The
Comedy of Job," in a forthcoming issue of *Semeia*.

> The less could I refute him,
> Or match words with him.
> Though innocent I would not reply;
> I would have to beg for mercy.
> . . . .
> Though guiltless, *my* mouth would declare me guilty.
> (9:13–15, 20a; my translation and italics)

Thus once more Job has been right. In 42:2–6 he has to entreat his opponent; in order to calm God's whirlwinds he has to declare his guilt by his own mouth. He makes his confession, then, tongue-in-cheek. This interpretation receives some support from the fact that Job in 42:2 confesses to nothing that he has not already admitted several times, that God is so powerful that no purpose of his can be thwarted.

The friends also speculate what God would do were he to appear to Job. Take Zophar's statement in 11:5–6, for example:

> But would that God might speak,
> Might open his lips against you.
> He would tell you what is hidden,
> For there are two sides to wisdom.

In other words, if God were to speak he would expose your ignorance, Job. And this is exactly what God tries to do, as we have seen. So not only is Job right in his predictions, but the friends are right in theirs. And if we let this agreement between the friends' wishes and God's performance lead us to meditate further on the relationship between God and the friends, some rather startling thoughts come to mind. For example, God seems to think in terms of the same either-or alternative that characterizes the friends' thinking about Job: either Job is innocent and God guilty, or Job is guilty and God innocent. And it is abundantly clear who God thinks is the guilty party:

> Will the contender with Shaddai yield?
> He who reproves God, let him answer for it.
> . . . .
> Would you annul my judgment,
> Condemn me that you may be justified? (40:2, 8)

Furthermore, God's attitude toward Job is identical to the friends' attitude toward him. Take, for example, God's words just quoted, or his opening words in chapter 38, "Who is this that denies Providence with words void of knowledge?" and compare them with any number of the friends' statements, such as the following:

> How long will you prate so?
> Your speech is so much wind. (8:2)

> Are you the first man ever born,
> Were you brought forth before the hills?
> Do you eavesdrop on the divine council,
> Do you hold a monopoly on wisdom? (15:7–8)

Not only is the tonality of God's remarks the same as the friends', but he likewise accuses Job of gross ignorance. We can conclude from these observations that God is the friends writ large, a cosmic Eliphaz, Bildad, and Zophar. And, our attitude toward the friends naturally transfers at this point to God, so that he like them is viewed by us as a false comforter.

Now we can also understand more fully the function of Elihu. He anticipates God's moves in almost every way. He assumes, as does God, that he is superior to Job. He, too, assumes that Job must be the guilty party. His speech is inflated, bombastic, as is God's. And he even anticipates (in 36:22ff.) God's own description of his technological prowess. And from Elihu all this is very laughable. Then when God appears and mimics Elihu in word and gesture and attitude, it becomes very difficult to view him reverently. Take a professor given to exaggerated oratory. Let a student mimic his mannerisms before he arrives. The class's reaction when he begins his lecture with the customary flourish is inevitable.

To sum up, now, the foregoing interpretation of God's speeches from the storm. We expect God to prove his own and Job's innocence. Yet apparently God has been so threatened by Job's accusations that he makes Job guilty in an attempt to prove that he is a just and wise God. But because he behaves as Job said he would, he fails to convince us of his justice and wisdom. In fact, he convinces us of precisely the opposite, and moreover, because he seems so much like the friends, persuades us that he is unloving as well as unjust and unwise.

THE RETURN TO THE PROSE STORY

We have seen that Job was right about God. As we return to the prose story we find that God himself admits that Job was right, for there we read the astounding statement by God:

After Yahweh had spoken these words to Job, Yahweh said to Eliphaz the Temanite, "My anger burns against you and your two friends; for you have not spoken truth of me, as did Job, my servant." (42:7)

The friends, who said that God does not pervert justice, are wrong! And Job, who said that God "mocks the despair of the innocent" (9:23), is right! Apparently the folk tale originally contained speeches by Job and the friends, but in these speeches Job argued that God is just, and the friends that he is unjust. In other words, their respective roles were exactly the opposite of their roles in the present book. In this context God's praise of Job and condemnation of the friends were appropriate. Once the present dialogues were substituted for the originals, however, God's praise of Job amounts to a terrible self-incrimination. Now his words in 42:7 mean exactly the opposite of what he wants and once intended them to mean. God is the object of an ironic joke. And after this bit of irreverence it is impossible for us to take seriously the solution to the problem of suffering offered by the folk tale—that the righteous man who suffers patiently will have his earthly goods doubled (which is, incidentally, the solution proposed by the three friends to Job). This is fairy tale comfort offered to a man in real pain.

THE MEANING OF JOB

Kenneth Burke in his book *The Philosophy of Literary Form* (New York, 1957) likens the poet to a medicine man who generally adopts one of two strategies to effect his cure. The malady is man's fear of fate, his destiny, the unknown. One poetic strategy is homeopathic—to effect a cure by prescribing more of that which is causing the disease. That is, the poet cures man of fear by inducing fear, but in such a way that man responds to the fear not with panic but with awe. This strategy Burke labels "the sublime," and cites *Oedipus Tyrannus* as a good example. The other strategy is to cure by antidote, that is, to cure fear by means of its opposite, ridicule of the object feared. We do not fear that which we feel beneath us in dignity; rather we scorn it. This is, as I see it, the strategy of the book of Job. While God may be more powerful than we are, he is beneath us on scales that measure love, justice, and wisdom. So we know of him what we know of all tyrants, that while they may torture us and finally kill us, they cannot destroy our personal integrity. From this fact we take our comfort.

IV

Lyric Poetry: Psalm 90 and "Hymn to Intellectual Beauty"

Erhard Gerstenberger in his instructive summary of form critical inquiries into the psalms[1] describes what psalm exegesis was like in the *ancien régime* of Wellhausen and Driver. In those days

most OT exegetes would look upon the Psalter . . . as a product of literary art. Each psalm was considered first and foremost the written proclamation of a poet. Focal points of interest, consequently, were, in the first place, the author's historical situation, the events and the environment to which he reacted in his poem, and secondly, his inner feelings, the psychological and religious condition he presumably lived in. Thus OT scholars between 1800 and 1920 mainly dedicated themselves to uncovering in each psalm traces of the history of Israel; and they were eager to learn how the psalmists had put their personal experiences of national affairs into words and poetic structures.

Then, around the turn of the century came the *religionsgeschichtliche Schule* and out of it came Gunkel and form criticism as the model by which virtually all Old Testament scholars conducted their research. Its proponents, considering the psalms not as products of literary art but as products of recurring social events, made some extraordinary discoveries and dramatically increased our knowledge of the meaning and use of biblical psalms in their original situation. While this chapter does not intend to call into question form critical procedures or findings, it does represent an attempt to leap backward over form criticism and once again consider the psalms primarily as literary art.

Even a cursory comparison of Chapter I with Gerstenberger's summary of pre-form critical literary analysis will show, however, that the questions likely to be asked in this chapter are quite different from

[Portions of this chapter originally appeared in *Semeia*, no. 8 (1977) and are reprinted with permission of the publisher.]
1. In *Old Testament Form Criticism*, ed. John H. Hayes, Trinity University Monographs in Religion, vol. 2 (San Antonio: Trinity University Press, 1974), p. 180.

those asked by literary scholars of the nineteenth century. They were mainly concerned with the sensibility of the poet as an individual, and used the psalm as a pathway into the poet's inner life. We, on the contrary, will be concerned with the psalm as literary object. Whether it was written by an individual or is a product of a community, as the form critics would have it, makes little difference. Once a psalm is published it begins to lose its connection with its author(s) and his (their) situation and takes on an independent life of its own. The passage of time and the association of the psalm with other literary documents (like the rest of the Old Testament or the Bible as a whole) further estrange it from its *Sitz im Leben*. Finally, as it takes its place beside all other literary artifacts in the grand body of literature, it becomes appropriate to consider it as one might consider any other work of literature. One can now apply to it categories that are used in the general study of literature, whether or not these categories were present in the culture in which it was written. And the conclusions reached by such study tell us, first of all, how it functions as a literary object, and only secondarily provide clues about how it was appropriated in its own time. In summary, the interest here is in the understanding gained by considering a psalm as any other lyric poem, say one by Sappho, or Wordsworth, or Eliot.

The aim of this chapter is very modest. It will focus on a single psalm, Psalm 90, and by considering it in relation to Shelley's "Hymn to Intellectual Beauty," attempt to demonstrate one way, and certainly not the only way, of construing a biblical poem as an aesthetic object. While Shelley's poem belongs to the same literary genre as Psalm 90 (the hymn), unlike Psalm 90 it has no connection with the cult, it was not composed primarily for oral recitation, and it was written by a single, identifiable, and acutely self-conscious poet. By juxtaposing Psalm 90 to it, I will try to show that the same type of literary analysis that produces significant results with works self-consciously written as literature produces equally significant results with poems originally written as part of the ongoing activities of a specific social institution and only later subsumed into the body of pure literature.

"HYMN TO INTELLECTUAL BEAUTY"

Coming to "Hymn to Intellectual Beauty" from a study of biblical psalms, one is immediately struck by the formal similarities between it and biblical complaint psalms.[2] It contains many of the formal

2. Some terminological confusion is bound to occur at this point. Biblical critics tend to use psalm to indicate genus and hymn to designate species. Thus, a hymn

elements said by form critics to be distinguishing characteristics of
complaint psalms: direct address to the deity followed by relative
clauses serving as epithets:

> Spirit of BEAUTY, that dost consecrate
> > With thine own hues all thou dost shine upon
> > Of human thought or form—where art thou gone?
> > > (lines 13–15)

definitions of the nature of the deity:

> > Thou messenger of sympathies,
> > That wax and wane in lovers' eyes—
> Thou—that to human thought art nourishment,
> > Like darkness to a dying flame!   (lines 42–45)

a rehearsal of god's past aid:

> While yet a boy I sought for ghosts, and sped
> > Through many a listening chamber, cave and ruin,
> > And starlight wood, with fearful steps pursuing
> Hopes of high talk with the departed dead.
> I called on poisonous names with which our youth is fed;
> > I was not heard—I saw them not—
> > When musing deeply on the lot
> Of life, at that sweet time when winds are wooing
> > All vital things that wake to bring
> > News of birds and blossoming—
> > Sudden, thy shadow fell on me;
> I shrieked, and clasped my hands in ecstasy!   (lines 49–60)

descriptions of the petitioner's plight:

> > Depart not as thy shadow came,
> > Depart not—lest the grave should be,
> Like life and fear, a dark reality.   (lines 47–48)

questions addressed to the deity:

> > > —where art thou gone?
> > Why doest thou pass away and leave our state,
> > This dim vast vale of tears, vacant and desolate?
> > > (lines 15–17)

protestations of the speaker's past loyalty:

> I vowed that I would dedicate my powers
> > To thee and thine—have I not kept the vow?
> > With beating heart and streaming eyes, even now

is a psalm of praise.   Literary critics, on the other hand, mean by hymn what
biblical critics mean by psalm.   In this chapter I follow the practice of literary
critics.   Hymn is the generic term, and species of this genre are designated by
adjectival or prepositional phrases (e.g., complaint hymn or hymn of complaint).

> I call the phantoms of a thousand hours
> Each from his voiceless grave: they have in visioned bowers
>   Of studious zeal or love's delight
>   Outwatched with me the envious night—
> They know that never joy illumed my brow
>   Unlinked with hope that thou wouldst free
>   This world from its dark slavery,
>   That thou—O awful LOVELINESS,
> Wouldst give whate'er these words cannot express.
>
> (lines 61–72)

and, finally, direct petition:

> Thus let thy power, which like the truth
>   Of nature on my passive youth
> Descended, to my onward life supply
>   Its calm—   (lines 78–80)

But, of course, in this case a cultic *Sitz im Leben* and group composition are out of the question. The most that a literary critic might do with this information is use it in locating the subcategory of the hymn to which "Hymn to Intellectual Beauty" belongs. He might even be anxious to borrow the term "complaint psalm" from the form critic, for certainly the poem's purpose seems to be to complain of Beauty's inconstancy and to secure Beauty's aid by motivating it to act on Shelley's[3] behalf. But while labeling "Hymn to Intellectual Beauty" a complaint psalm may not be inaccurate, it is superficial and misleading.

Crucial to any complaint psalm is the speaker's confidence in his god, and, therefore, in the efficacy of the ritual he engages in while reciting the psalm. He knows that his god is near and eventually will act on

---

3. Literary critics like myself, who are mainly concerned with the internal dynamics of a poem rather than with the interior of the poet's mind, have found it helpful to distinguish between the persona who speaks the poem (the "I" of "Hymn to Intellectual Beauty") and the poem's author (the man, Percy Bysshe Shelley). Some critics, to emphasize this distinction, use the term "the poet" to refer to the speaking persona and, by this means, avoid completely using the author's name when writing about the poem. Others, among whom I include myself, find exclusive use of the term "the poet" rather awkward in an extended essay. They also believe that what can and ought to be distinguished (that is, the author and his poem) need not be divorced from each other. So while they may not wish to use the poem as an avenue into the poet's life and times, they may want to use his life and times, if known, as background for understanding the poem. I have, therefore, used Shelley's name to indicate the speaking persona of "Hymn to Intellectual Beauty," fully aware of the ambiguities this practice raises. Certain kinds of ambiguity are probably quite helpful, since they remind us of the limits of our attempts to put either life or literature into neatly separable logical boxes. Also, below, I turn to Shelley's prose essay, A *Defence of Poetry*, as relevant background material for understanding his poem.

his behalf. Shelley, on the contrary, seems to have lost confidence in his deity's accessibility. For him Beauty is extremely remote. He thinks of it as light. To be sure, only a poet overconfident of his deity's accessibility would claim that he sees the light directly. Surely, however, a confident poet would at least claim that he sees a reflection of that light. But for Shelley Beauty's light is not seen at all. Furthermore, although its light casts a shadow, not even this shadow is seen:

> The awful shadow of some unseen Power
> Floats though unseen among us—   (lines 1–2)

Therefore, not only is he two removes from the light, but he is, as it were, two negative removes from it. A light casts a shadow (first negative remove, negative because the shadow defines where the light is not) which is unseen (second negative remove).

The similes Shelley uses to describe Beauty's visitation reinforce the idea of its remoteness by suggesting how extremely tenuous is its epiphany:

> —visiting
> This various world with as inconstant wing
> As summer winds that creep from flower to flower—
> Like moonbeams that behind some piny mountain shower,
> It visits with inconstant glance
> Each human heart and countenance;
> Like hues and harmonies of evening—
> Like clouds in starlight widely spread—
>   (lines 2–9)

> Thy light alone—like mist o'er mountains driven,
> Or music by the night wind sent
> Through strings of some still instrument,
> Or moonlight on a midnight stream,
> Gives race and truth to life's unquiet dream.
>   (lines 32–36)

Because Beauty is manifest only as an unseen shadow, Shelley resorts partially to images drawn from senses other than sight to explain its appearance. Whether these images are kinesthetic (floating), tactile (wind), or auditory (music), they refer to things which have an airiness about them, which are often difficult to perceive (especially if the winds be summer winds creeping and the music be from a still instrument), momentary, gone as quickly and as furtively as they came. And when he does use visual imagery, the figures paradoxically either reinforce the shadowy nature of the epiphany or suggest restricted visibility. Thus, Beauty's self-manifestation is like "clouds in starlight," which would appear to an observer like huge shadows defined by the stars around the edges, or like the "hues and harmonies of evening."

Moreover, the concatenation of similes further reinforces Beauty's remoteness by leading us away from sense experience. Each image in the first list (lines 2–9) by itself tends to take us imaginatively to the lowest threshold of sense perception. "Summer winds that creep" are barely feelable, and "moonbeams that behind some piny mountain shower" and "clouds in starlight" are barely seeable. And the images taken serially attempt to loosen further our already tenuous grasp on the material world by leading up to the last simile. Beauty's shadow visits us "like memory of music fled" (line 10). Music is a sensory stimulus, but of the most ethereal kind. Reduce its materiality even further by having it not experienced but remembered, and one approximates a purely mental event. Thus, stanza 1 begins with Beauty manifest as an unseen shadow, a mystery, and the similes employed to clarify lead to the conclusion that it is a mystery still:

> Like aught that for its grace may be
> Dear, and yet dearer for its mystery.   (lines 11–12)

Because Beauty is so remote from Shelley, it is not at his disposal. A complaint hymn presupposes that the deity addressed is movable. But Shelley has no confidence that anything he says or does will alter its mode of relating to this world. Its epiphanies are as inconstant as the winds. It passes away and leaves us destitute:

> Why dost thou pass away and leave our state,
> This dim vast vale of tears, vacant and desolate?
>   (lines 16–17)

And Shelley is powerless to alter this state of affairs. His helplessness is reflected even in the simile that he uses to express its inconstancy: when the wind will caress the flowers or the strings of the Aeolian harp is beyond human control.

The most direct statement of man's powerlessness to change Beauty's relationship to the world comes in stanza 2. If you wish to know why it is inconstant, Shelley says to the reader, you should ask:

> . . . why the sunlight not forever
> Weaves rainbows o'er yon mountain river,
> Why aught should fail and fade that once is shown,
>   Why fear and dream and death and birth
>   Cast on the daylight of this earth
>   Such gloom—why man has such a scope
> For love and hate, despondency and hope?   (lines 18–24)

The effect of these questions upon the reader is to associate Beauty's inconstancy with the conditions of human existence. These conditions consist of pairs of opposites: fear in contrast with dream, death in contrast with birth, love in contrast with hate, and despondency in contrast with hope. In context these pairs are associated with another pair: Beauty's fleeting visitations in contrast with its long periods of absence. And just as man can do nothing to alter the former conditions, he can do nothing to alter the latter. Beauty's as well as love's inconstancy is a given.

Because Beauty is so inconstant and so inaccessible, what it can do for Shelley is, in the final analysis, minimal. What he wishes it would do is clear: convert the night of fear and death to daylight:

> Thou messenger of sympathies,
> That wax and wane in lovers' eyes—
> Thou—that to human thought art nourishment,
> Like darkness to a dying flame!
> Depart not as thy shadow came,
> Depart not—lest the grave should be,
> Like life and fear, a dark reality.   (lines 42–48)

or do what religion has been unable to do, free us from "doubt, chance, and mutability":

> No voice from some sublimer world hath ever
> To sage or poet these responses given—
> Therefore the names of Demon, Ghost, and Heaven,
> Remain the records of their vain endeavor,
> Frail spells—whose uttered charm might not avail to sever,
> From all we hear and all we see,
> Doubt, chance, and mutability.   (lines 25–31)

And it seems clear that Beauty in itself has the power to accomplish these things. If it were not so inconstant, man would be immortal and omnipotent:

> Man were immortal, and omnipotent,
> Didst thou, unknown and awful as thou art,
> Keep with thy glorious train firm state within his heart.
>   (lines 39–41)

But while the conditional clause contains some cause for hope (Beauty might become less inconstant) it contains much greater cause for despondency. Although it appears that it might do more for mankind if it would only decide to do so, actually what it does do and what it will and can do are the same. As the association of its capriciousness with the antipodal conditions of existence in lines 18–24 shows, its inconstancy is one of the fixtures of existence and is no more likely to change than the other conditions are.

What, then, can Beauty do for Shelley? It can only give life a grace. Both times this word occurs in the poem it immediately follows a list of sensory images (see lines 4–12 and 32–36 quoted above). In this context it takes on, as its primary meaning, a quality added to things, not a power gratuitously bestowed on man by a deity. Beauty's light adds the type of quality to life that moonbeams and music add to a scene. In short, Beauty functions as does the human imagination. In his A *Defence of Poetry* Shelley says:

According to one mode of regarding those two classes of mental action, which are called reason and imagination, the former may be considered as mind contemplating the relations borne by one thought to another, however produced; and the latter, as mind acting upon those thoughts so as to colour them with its own light . . .[4]

Likewise, Beauty's epiphany gives evening its "hues and harmonies" (line 8), and later it is described as one that

> dost consecrate
> With thine own hues all thou dost shine upon
> Of human thought or form—   (lines 13–15)

Thus, what Beauty can do for mankind is only to give things a coloring, suffuse them with loveliness.

At the beginning of this discussion of "Hymn to Intellectual Beauty" we saw that it ostensibly is a hymn of complaint. Yet, we now see that Beauty's inaccessibility and relative powerlessness seem to make any complaint futile. This tension is the key to understanding what is happening in the poem. Rather than persuade Beauty to be less inconstant, the poem consoles the poet and reader for the fact that it is and forever will be inconstant. The poet is talking to himself far more importantly than he is addressing it. The crucial question is, I think, what allows him to end the poem on a note of calm? It is not hope in Beauty's help, or assurance that it will somehow change its nature in the future. Rather, the calm he achieves depends on something else entirely, or to be more specific, on two other things.

First, Shelley is able to end his poem all calm because of the consolation that comes with the imposition of aesthetic form. Writing a poem is itself an aesthetic strategy! According to that strategy, ordered words have a power to produce a corresponding order within the self. Shelley says in A *Defence of Poetry*: "It is impossible to feel

---

4. P. B. Shelley, *Selected Poems, Essays, and Letters*, ed. Ellsworth Barnard (New York: Odyssey Press), p. 529.

them [the verses of Provençal Trouveurs] without becoming a portion of that beauty which we contemplate . . ." and elsewhere: "The frequent recurrence of the poetical power, it is obvious to suppose, may produce in the mind a habit of order and harmony correlative with its own nature and with its effects upon other minds."[5] The working premise in "Hymn to Intellectual Beauty" seems to be that the expression of a disordering emotion (in this case, despair and the anxiety it causes) in a controlling medium allows the poet to come to terms with that emotion.

Of more interest, however, are the aesthetic devices Shelley uses within the poem to induce calm. He chooses, for example, a very demanding stanzaic form (twelve iambic lines, the first four of which are pentameter, the fifth hexameter, the next six tetrameter, and the last pentameter, with rhyme scheme abbaaccbddee) and invariably adheres to that form. In addition, he tries to impose aesthetic form on the conditions of existence through the poetic rehearsal of those conditions. In the final stanza he returns, after a two stanza narrative of his own personal history, to the declarative recitation of the conditions of existence that characterized much of the first four stanzas. But in these stanzas such recitation invariably led to a wish that the conditions were other than they are.

In the final stanza the recitation leads nowhere; it is an end in itself just as autumn is an end in itself:

> The day becomes more solemn and serene
> When noon is past—there is harmony
> In autumn, and a luster in its sky,
> Which through the summer is not heard or seen,
> As if it could not be, as if it had not been!
> (lines 73–77)

Autumn is accepted as autumn, which as prelude to winter is symbolic of death, precisely that which Shelley wants most to wish away in the preceding stanzas. And there is an implicit rejection of the wish that life were all summer, which as the sequel to spring is symbolic of eternal day, of the wish that death-bound life would flower into eternal life. Now the petition to Beauty is not that it would save him from bondage to death, but that it will enable him to live calmly this life-in-death:

> Thus let thy power, which like the truth
> Of nature on my passive youth
> Descended, to my onward life supply
> Its calm—   (lines 78–81)

5. Ibid., pp. 552 and 566.

In other words, the recitation in stanza 7 represents a change from a wish that the conditions of existence were other than they are to an acceptance of them as they are. Emblematic of this acceptance is the modulation of the imagery of darkness and night used to describe the human condition in the first six stanzas to the somber but also serene and deep colors of evening and autumn of the final stanzas.

Along with the imposition of aesthetic form goes an attempt to gain wisdom, consisting of two movements. The first is a matter of seeing a glory in human life that could not be if the conditions of existence were wished away. Autumn symbolizes this glory: take away "doubt, chance, mutability" and man's autumn never arrives—there is only perpetual summer—and if autumn never arrives, its solemnity, serenity, and luster never arrive. The second consists of the deduction of morality from ontology. For Shelley is and ought are correlative. Beauty's epiphany revealed to him its essential nature. In stanza 7 he attempts to draw the appropriate moral conclusion: you ought to fear yourself (fear here meaning "hold in awe, esteem") and love your fellow man:

> Whom, SPIRIT fair, thy spells did bind
> To fear himself, and love all human kind.   (lines 83–84)

These maxims translate into practical duties, the execution of which is in Shelley's power, whereas fellowship with Beauty is beyond his power. The movement from the latter to the former illustrates perfectly the essence of the strategy of consolation: a turning from what man cannot do to what he can do.

PSALM 90

We can say, on the basis of form criticism, that Psalm 90 too is a hymn of complaint, though for a community rather than an individual to sing. We find a direct address to God (v. 1), definitions of his nature (vv. 2–6), a statement of his aid to the community in the past (v. 1) and a description of the community's plight (vv. 13–17). As with "Hymn to Intellectual Beauty," however, the label "complaint psalm" may cause us to misconstrue Psalm 90's actual literary strategy.

Note first how removed, how inaccessible God seems. He is so very exalted and mankind so very lowly. This distance between them is expressed in terms of time and holiness. Nowhere in all of literature are God's eternity and man's transiency more poignantly contrasted than in vv. 2–6:

> Before the mountains were brought forth,
>> or ever thou hadst formed the earth and the world,
>> from everlasting to everlasting thou art God.
> Thou turnest man back to the dust,
>> and sayest, "Turn back, O children of men!"
> For a thousand years in thy sight
>> are but as yesterday when it is past,
>> or as a watch in the night.
> Thou dost sweep men away; they are like a dream
>> like grass which is renewed in the morning:
> in the morning it flourishes and is renewed;
>> in the evening it fades and withers.

And in the next three verses this overwhelming disparity between God and man is related to the disparity in holiness:

> For we are consumed by thy anger;
>> by thy wrath we are overwhelmed.
> Thou hast set our iniquities before thee,
>> our secret sins in the light of thy countenance,
> For all our days pass away under thy wrath,
>> our years come to an end like a sigh.
> The years of our life are threescore and ten,
>> or even by reason of strength fourscore;
> yet their span is but toil and trouble;
>> they are soon gone, and we fly away.   (vv. 7–10)

What is perhaps most impressive about the conditions described in these verses is their permanence. These differences between God and the human species are essential, not contingent. The community is not setting forth temporary dislocations in the rightful order of things that they could ask God to set straight, like military defeats, natural disasters, droughts, or plagues. Rather they are describing the way things have been, are, and always will be. They cannot and do not, therefore, ask God to change them, just as Shelley does not really ask Beauty to be less inconstant, knowing full well that its inconstancy is part of the way things are. Much the way he asked that life's dark realities be sometimes filtered through the romantic imagination, they ask only that the weight of life's conditions on their shoulders be eased somewhat:

> Return, O LORD! How long?
>> Have pity on thy servants!
> Satisfy us in the morning with thy steadfast love,
>> that we may rejoice and be glad all our days.
> Make us glad as many days as thou hast afflicted us,
>> and as many years as we have seen evil.   (vv. 13–15)

Thus, Psalm 90 differs dramatically from most complaint psalms in its description of the conditions that occasion the complaint. Whereas in the latter impermanent, and so remediable, situations are recounted, in Psalm 90 we find a permanent, and so irremediable, situation. This difference signals a loss of confidence in the very ritual the community is engaging in. For the community to gather in worship to sing a complaint psalm, they need to believe that God can and will alter the circumstances that give rise to the complaint. Yet in this case no possibility exists that God could or would alter the state of affairs expressed in verses 2–10. It would seem, then, that Psalm 90 is a poem of ultimate despair, in which a people need to ask for that which they know they cannot get.

Yet, the experience of virtually all readers of this psalm testifies to the fact that it is not a poem of despair. Most readers experience a calm at the end, even a kind of exhilaration, tempered, to be sure, by the somber mood of the poem. And, as with "Hymn to Intellectual Beauty," the crucial question is this: what brings about this calm? Not God, or belief in his imminent or even delayed intervention on behalf of his people, or trust in the efficacy of the liturgy the community is engaging in. Rather the poem itself, by its own means, accomplishes this end. And its means are the same two strategies we found in "Hymn to Intellectual Beauty." First, calm comes to the reader because of the wisdom he has gained. In verses 11–12 the community asks for God to teach them wisdom:

> Who considers the power of thy anger,
>   and thy wrath according to the fear of thee?
> So teach us to number our days
>   that we may get a heart of wisdom.

Actually, he has already done so, and the community expresses what they have learned in verses 2–10. In other words, the psalm consists, for the most part, in the expression of the collective wisdom of the community. And it is important to note that this wisdom is not knowledge of how better to cope with the world instrumentally, as the wisdom of Proverbs is—how to get and stay rich, how to keep God on your side, etc. Rather, it consists of the knowledge of the facts of life as the community sees them: God's utter transcendence and man's utter abjection.

But these are hard facts. Why would they comfort? Here is where the second means of finding consolation comes into play: the imposition of aesthetic form. The community finds that a poetic recitation of the facts of human existence, that is, verses 2–10, helps them gain distance from these facts, and so helps them to accept them, however harsh they may be. The literary premise here seems to be that there is a peculiar power in aesthetically ordered words to produce a corresponding order in the self.

Compare, for example, Gen. 3:19:

> In the sweat of your face
>   you shall eat bread
> till you return to the ground,
>   for out of it you were taken;
> you are dust,
>   and to dust you shall return.

This is a curse, but to state it poetically is to take a step in the direction of bearing it. Adam is supposed to be crushed by God's curse, yet it is doubtful that any man has ever read these words without taking an immense, deep satisfaction in his own participation in the cycle of from dust to dust. It is the same with Psalm's 90's "threescore and ten, or even by reason of strength fourscore." It seems true of mankind that to impose aesthetic form on the most unconsoling facts helps in finding consolation for them. In some strange way cataloguing poetically the conditions of existence helps condition us to them. Psalm 90 ends:

> Let the favor of the LORD our God be upon us,
>   and establish thou the work of our hands upon us,
> yea, the work of our hands establish thou it.   (v. 17)

The repetition of the last line with subtle changes in the rhythm is an aesthetic device used here with consummate skill. Its effect may be compared with the effect of the progression from dominant to tonic in music. A resolution of tension, a feeling of finality, comes from the very sound of the words.

To sum up, then, Psalm 90, like "Hymn to Intellectual Beauty," is formally a hymn of complaint but functionally a hymn of consolation. The Israelite community knows what Shelley knows, that no petition from them is going to lead God to make human life basically any different. A profound despair, therefore, informs their singing, and leads them to alter subtly the purpose of the hymn they compose. Since help from their God is not forthcoming, and since they cannot materially affect their fate without his help, they attempt to help themselves by such devices as are available. They are in need of composing themselves in the face of the threats existence poses, threats now more terrible without assurance of God's aid. As a result, they address their hymn not so much to God as their own souls, and its purpose is more fundamentally to console themselves than to motivate God.

PURE VERSUS APPLIED LITERATURE

The above reading of Psalm 90 is a result of taking it primarily as an aesthetic rather than as a religious object. In the context of this book taking a text as an aesthetic object means, first and foremost, that we focus our attention on its internal verbal dynamics, that is, on the play of words on the page, on the patterns and movements that the words create and on the shape and content of the thoughts and emotions aroused in us the readers by those words. Thus, one way of stating the difference between pure literature and religious literature (as one species of applied literature) might go as follows: pure literature relies primarily on the manipulation of words for its effects on our thoughts and emotions, and secondarily on the particular ideas expressed by those words, whereas the opposite is the case with religious literature. This thesis, of course, is not by any means universally accepted, but an abundance of evidence can be cited to support it. For example, *Oedipus Tyrannus* remains one of the most powerful plays ever written, although I doubt if one could find a single reader today who would assent to its particular ideas about the gods and their activities.

Similarly, as here interpreted, the thoughts and emotions we experience when reading Psalm 90 are brought about primarily by literary means, and so are essentially independent of religious beliefs. One need be neither Jew nor Christian, nor even a theist, to experience the calm it achieves.

It is possible to test this hypothesis by comparing with Psalm 90 a psalm with significant religious content but with less literary merit. Psalm 73 can serve as an example. Verses 1–14 set up the problem. The psalmist believes that God rewards the righteous and punishes the wicked, but he has also noticed the comfort and affluence of many a wicked man. This discrepancy between belief and experience has created in him a great anxiety, an anxiety that he communicates to the reader rather successfully. By verse 14 the reader too is likely feeling anxious:

> Truly God is good to the upright,
> to those who are pure in heart.
> But as for me, my feet had almost stumbled,
> my steps had well nigh slipped.

> For I was envious of the arrogant,
>> when I saw the prosperity of the wicked.
> For they have no pangs;
>> their bodies are sound and sleek.
> They are not in trouble as other men are;
>> they are not stricken like other men.
> Therefore pride is their necklace;
>> violence covers them as a garment.
> Their eyes swell out with fatness,
>> their hearts overflow with follies.
> They scoff and speak with malice;
>> loftily they threaten oppression.
> They set their mouths against the heavens,
>> and their tongue struts through the earth.
> Therefore the people turn and praise them;
>> and find no fault in them.
> And they say, "How can God know?
>> Is there knowledge in the Most High?"
> Behold, these are the wicked;
>> always at ease, they increase in riches.
> All in vain have I kept my heart clean
>> and washed my hands in innocence.
> For all the day long I have been stricken,
>> and chastened every morning.   (vv. 1–14)

In the next six verses he reports how his anxiety was allayed:

> If I had said, "I will speak thus,"
>> I would have been untrue to the generation of thy children.
> But when I thought how to understand this,
>> it seemed to me a wearisome task,
> until I went into the sanctuary of God;
>> then I perceived their end.
> Truly thou dost set them in slippery places;
>> thou dost make them fall to ruin.
> How they are destroyed in a moment,
>> swept away utterly by terrors!
> They are like a dream when one awakes,
>> on awaking you despise their phantoms.

The psalmist has had some sort of ecstatic vision in the temple, the intellectual content of which was the revelation that the wicked get their punishment in the end.

The crucial question for our purposes is this: what about the reader's anxiety, is it calmed by these six verses? Most likely the reader is calmed only if he shares the psalmist's belief that the wicked finally get their just desserts. The words of the psalm, unlike the words in Shelley's poem or in Psalm 90, do not, by their very arrangement on the page, lead the thoughts and emotions of the reader through the ecstasy of the vision to an emotional calm on the other side. They do little more than report that a vision took place and summarize the intellectual content of that vision.

The words of Psalm 73 are pointers. If you have been down that road, you can follow their directions. If you have not, you will likely remain lost despite the signposts. The words of Psalm 90, on the other hand, generate in us the experience itself, control our responses, and bring us out on the other side all calm. They do not point to a journey, they are the journey.

V

The Prophets as Poets

Not only does the Bible contain texts that, taken individually, are great pieces of literature, but it itself can be considered as a single, monumental work of art. And in this work the idea of the word of God plays a major role. The content of God's word, the promise of nationhood to Abraham's descendants, of deliverance to the slaves in Egypt, of restoration to the exiles, and so forth, is one of the Bible's magnificent themes. Yet, interestingly enough, because in the New Testament the word of God becomes a man, it is also, quite literally, an aspect of the Bible's plot. This chapter is concerned with the process by which spoken word becomes living person. Although we will begin with Yahweh's promise to Abraham, most of the chapter will be devoted to the four major writing prophets, Isaiah, Jeremiah, Ezekiel, and Second Isaiah.

But, first, a caveat is in order. None of the statements in this chapter is to be understood as referring to history, that is, to what actually happened in Palestine between roughly 1500 B.C. and 100 A.D. The sole concern here is with the story as narrated in the Bible. Thus, when, say, a claim is made about Isaiah, that claim refers not to the historical Isaiah but to Isaiah as a dramatis persona in a book construed as fiction rather than as history. That is, the book of Isaiah is being taken here as a work of fiction, and no judgment is being made one way or the other about the reliability of the data reported therein.

The foregoing remarks are important since the subject-matter of this chapter (roughly speaking, the development of Old Testament prophecy and its fulfillment in the New Testament) is a common theme of historical and theological writing about the Bible. One might think, therefore, that the criteria for making judgments in this chapter are also historical and/or theological, and that, consequently, the literary perspective has been forsaken. Such is not the case. One of the reasons for this chapter is to show how a subject traditionally approached from historical and theological perspectives might be handled from a literary point of view. Study of institutions (in this case, prophecy) and ideas (in this case, the fulfillment of prophecy in Jesus) that occur in texts taken as fiction is as important as the study of character, plot, and language.

An example may help clarify the angle of vision on prophecy taken in this chapter. The setting of Faulkner's novels is Yoknapatawpha County. A literary critic might well attempt to write a history of this county, and in so doing he would chart the development not only of individuals and families but also of institutions (like slavery) and ideas (like the concept of the wilderness). In carrying out this project all his evidence would necessarily come from within the texts themselves. Charting the course of prophecy in the Bible, once it is taken as literature, is exactly parallel to the literary critic's history of slavery in Yoknapatawpha County. Correspondingly, an attempt by an American historian to reconstruct the history of Lafayette County in Mississippi (the model for Faulkner's county), using Faulkner's novels as part of his evidence, parallels the biblical historian's effort to reconstruct the actual course of Israelite prophecy from the evidence given in the biblical texts. Only in these latter two cases would the reliability of Faulkner's novels or the Bible come into question.

Yahweh's initial word to his people was a promise to Abraham to make his descendants into a great nation:

Now the LORD said to Abram, "Go from your country and your kindred and your father's house to the land that I will show you. And I will make of you a great nation, and I will bless you, and make your name great, so that you will be a blessing." (Gen. 12:1–2)

on land that he, Yahweh, would give them:

On that day the LORD made a covenant with Abram, saying, "To your descendants I give this land, from the river of Egypt to the great river, the river Euphrates, the land of the Kenites, the Kenizzites, and Kadmonites, the Hittites, the Perizzites, the Rephaim, the Amorites, the Canaanites, the Girgashites and the Jebusites." (Gen. 15:18–21)

The first six books of the Bible (Genesis through Joshua) tell of the circuitous route Abraham's descendants take on their way to final possession of this land. At the end of the book of Joshua, one part of Yahweh's promise is fulfilled. Judges through 2 Samuel tell the story of the growth of a nation, culminating in the dynastic promise to David. With the reigns of David and Solomon, both parts of Yahweh's original twofold promise to Abraham have been fulfilled.

The fortune of God's people, however, ran rather precipitously downhill after Solomon, and at an ever increasing angle of descent. To make a long story short, the rise of two great Leviathans, Assyria and Babylonia, called God's promise to Abraham into question. The community had once, in the halcyon days of David and Solomon, possessed all the land promised to them. Now they were losing it. Back then the people were a house united, now they were divided into a northern and southern duplex. Then it seemed that the people had obeyed the commandments of Yahweh, but now they grew more and more corrupt. Somehow the old word had lost its power; it no longer spoke to the actual situation the community found itself in. A new word was needed and the prophets rose to speak it. Their word was double-edged. On the one hand, they uttered oracles of doom: they announced that the Assyrians and Babylonians were instruments of Yahweh's anger sent to punish Israel for its sins. But, on the other hand, they proclaimed oracles of hope: Yahweh was only punishing Israel; his final aim was purification not obliteration. He would in the end defeat all its enemies and make them its subjects, and, so that the cycle of sin-punishment-restoration would not be repeated, he would write his covenant not on stone but on the hearts of his people (Jer. 31:31–34) and would raise up a king who would establish peace and justice in the land (Isa. 11:1–5). Israel restored would be Paradise regained (cf. Isa. 11:6–9). In other words, the prophets considered as a group heralded a divine deed so radically new that it would, in effect, cancel out the old promise and constitute the community on a new foundation.

The overwhelming tragedy of Israel's story as told in 1 and 2 Kings and the prophetic books is that by and large only the oracles of doom came true. And, because the oracles of hope were not fulfilled, the prophetic word as a whole could not be regarded as self-fulfilling, although it was supposed to be. As the word of Yahweh it presumably had the power to bring about the event prophesied. But experience taught the hard lesson that words of hope were seemingly empty when Israel most wanted them full of power.

The prophetic response to this situation is what this chapter is concerned to discuss. In brief, the contention here is that the impotence of the prophetic word announcing imminent salvation is compensated for by a striking and momentous development: gradually, over a long period of time, from Amos through the servant figure in Second Isaiah to Jesus, the prophetic word comes veritably to constitute the event of which it speaks. When word pointed to event, experience showed that fulfillment might be indefinitely delayed. If word is event, however, then fulfillment is simultaneous with the act of speaking. The transformation from word as pointer to word as the thing itself is an extremely complicated process, as might be imagined, and can be observed in the lives of the prophets, as they are reported to us, as well as in their writings. The process seems to consist of three basic movements that happen more or less simultaneously. For clarity's sake we will discuss them sequentially.[1]

PERSON AND OFFICE

The theme of the first movement is the gradual collapse of the distinction between person and office. That is, over time we note a closer and closer identification between the prophet considered as an individual and the office he is called by Yahweh to perform. With Amos, virtually a complete separation between person and office exists. He is not a prophet by profession but a shepherd and a dresser of sycamore trees (Amos 1:1 and 7:14). Yahweh calls him during his adult life to preach to Israel and he obeys. Before long the king sends an emissary commanding him to cease prophesying. Although the narrator gives us no specific information on the matter, presumably Amos soon afterward returns to Tekoa to rejoin his fellow shepherds there.

Hosea and Isaiah are more closely identified with their office as prophet. Both use aspects of their private lives to speak Yahweh's word: Hosea makes his marriage into a parabolic sign of Yahweh's relation to Israel,[2] and both prophets turn their children's names into prophetic messages (Hos. 1–3, Isa. 7:3 and 8:1–4). In addition, Isaiah is intimately involved over a long period of time in the political events of his day, and it seems clear that in all his audiences with Judean monarchs he functions as prophet and not as private citizen. Yet, Isaiah like Amos is an adult when called by Yahweh to be a prophet (Isa. 7), and, more importantly, it is possible for him to take off the prophetic mantle and, at least temporarily, retire (Isa. 8:16ff.).

For Jeremiah and Ezekiel, a century later, the identification between person and office is complete. Yahweh says to Jeremiah:

---

1. The discussion that follows is indebted to Gerhard von Rad's treatment of prophecy in his *Old Testament Theology*, vol. II, trans. D. M. G. Stalker (New York: Harper & Row, 1965), especially pp. 188–262.

2. Note that, when the Bible is read as literature, we need not decide whether the details of chapters 1 and 3 of Hosea are fact or fiction. The literary meaning is the same in either case.

> Before I formed you in the womb I knew you,
> and before you were born I consecrated you;
> I appointed you a prophet to the nations.   (Jer. 1:5)

Not "after you were grown I called you" or "when you were a child," but "before you were born." Jeremiah comes from the womb as prophet already. To use philosophical terms that were foreign to Jeremiah yet express rather well his situation: being a prophet was not an accidental part of his being, it was his essence. No longer is the prophetic office a role from which he can more or less separate himself in his private life (as some priest today might leave his clerical robes behind as he departs with his family on vacation).

Jeremiah has no private life:

You shall not take a wife, nor shall you have sons or daughters in this place. For thus says the LORD concerning the sons and daughters who are born in this place, and concerning the mothers who bore them and the fathers who begot them in this land: They shall die of deadly diseases. (Jer. 16:2–3)

For thus says the LORD: Do not enter the house of mourning, or go to lament, or bemoan them; for I have taken away my peace from this people, says the LORD, my steadfast love and mercy. . . . You shall not go into the house of feasting to sit with them, to eat and drink. For thus says the LORD of hosts, the God of Israel: Behold, I will make to cease from this place, before your eyes and in your days, the voice of mirth and the voice of gladness, the voice of bridegroom and the voice of the bride. (Jer. 16:5, 8–9)

Furthermore, he cannot resign his office, even if he most desperately wants to:

> If I say, "I will not mention him,
>   or speak any more in his name,"
> there is in my heart as it were a burning fire
>   shut up in my bones,
> and I am weary with holding it in,
>   and I cannot.   (Jer. 20:9)

These same generalizations apply to Ezekiel, although he is, temperamentally and theologically, so different from Jeremiah. Take the following passage for instance:

Son of man, I have made you a watchman for the house of Israel; whenever you hear a word from my mouth, you shall give them warning from me. If I say to the wicked, "You shall surely die," and you give him no warning, nor speak to warn the wicked from his wicked way, in order to save his life, that wicked man shall die in his iniquity; but his blood I will require at your hand. But if you warn the wicked, and he does not turn from his wickedness, or from his wicked way, he shall die in his iniquity; but you will have saved your life. Again, if a righteous man turns from his righteousness and commits iniquity, and I lay a stumbling block before him, he shall die; because you have not warned him, he shall die for his sin, and his righteous deeds which he has done shall not be remembered; but his blood I will require at your hand. Nevertheless if you warn the righteous man not to sin, and he does not sin, he shall surely live, because he took warning; and you will have saved your life. (Ezek. 3:17–21)

What an incredible responsibility, whose execution would hardly leave Ezekiel a moment to himself! One is tempted to say that Ezekiel is so totally God's messenger that God can delegate to him responsibilities ordinarily considered to be God's and God's alone. Or, again, take another passage:

Also the word of the Lord came to me: "Son of man, behold, I am about to take the delight of your eyes away from you at a stroke; yet you shall not mourn or weep nor shall your tears run down. Sigh, but not aloud; make no mourning for the dead. Bind on your turban, and put your shoes on your feet; do not cover your lips, nor eat the bread of mourners." So I spoke to the people in the morning, and at evening my wife died. And on the next morning I did as I was commanded. (Ezek. 24:15–18)

The invasion of God into Ezekiel's private life could hardly be more complete.

PERSON AND WORD

The second movement in this symphony of the effective word consists of the gradual union of person and word. This process can perhaps best be seen in action in the call narratives of Isaiah, Jeremiah, and Ezekiel.

In the year that King Uzziah died I saw the Lord sitting upon a throne, high and lifted up; and his train filled the temple. Above him stood the seraphim; each had six wings: with two he covered his face, and with two he covered his feet, and with two he flew. And one called to another and said:
"Holy, holy, holy is the Lord of hosts;
    the whole earth is full of his glory."
And the foundations of the thresholds shook at the voice of him who called, and the house was filled with smoke. And I said: "Woe is me! For I am lost; for I am a man of unclean lips, and I dwell in the midst of a people of unclean lips; for my eyes have seen the King, the Lord of hosts!"
Then flew one of the seraphim to me, having in his hand a burning coal which he had taken with tongs from the altar. And he touched my mouth, and said, "Behold, this has touched your lips; your guilt is taken away, and your sin forgiven." And I heard the voice of the Lord saying, "Whom shall I send, and who will go for us?" Then I said, "Here I am! Send me." And he said, "Go, and say to this people:
            'Hear and hear, but do not understand;
            see and see, but do not perceive.'
        Make the heart of this people fat,

> and their ears heavy,
> and shut their eyes;
> lest they see with their eyes,
> and hear with their ears,
> and understand with their hearts,
> and turn and be healed." (Isa. 6:1–10)

The interplay of the senses is extremely interesting in this passage.
Isaiah is in jeopardy because he sees Yahweh on his throne. Yet, the
fault lies not with the eyes, but with the lips (important in this passage
not so much because they are the instrument for taking in food, but
because they are the instrument for giving forth language). There
the contagion lies. The idea is that what comes out of them makes
one unholy, so that sin and speaking wrongly of Yahweh are implicitly
equated. Such an emphasis on the lips is perhaps not surprising for
one whose office is that of spokesman for Yahweh. It is appropriate,
therefore, that the angel touches his lips with the hot coal, rather
than, say, his eyes or ears, or even his heart. Once his lips have been
cleansed, his ears open and he listens in on the divine assembly. After
he has volunteered for duty, Yahweh communicates the messages
Isaiah is to deliver in the usual manner, from the lips of Yahweh to
the ears of Isaiah.

Now listen to Jeremiah:

> Now the word of the Lord came to me saying,
> "Before I formed you in the womb I knew you,
> and before you were born I consecrated you;
> I appointed you a prophet to the nations."
> Then I said, "Ah, LORD God! Behold, I do not know how to
> speak, for I am only a youth." But the LORD said to me,
> "Do not say, 'I am only a youth';
> for to all to whom I send you you shall go,
> and whatever I command you you shall speak.
> Be not afraid of them,
> for I am with you to deliver you," says the LORD.
> Then the LORD put forth his hand and touched my mouth; and
> the LORD said to me,
> "Behold, I have put my words in your mouth.
> See, I have set you this day over nations and over kingdoms,
> to pluck up and to break down,
> to destroy and to overthrow,
> to build and to plant." (Jer. 1:4–10)

What impresses us immediately is the greater intimacy Jeremiah has
with Yahweh. He was made a prophet before he was even conceived.
No acute consciousness of sin is present to separate him from Yahweh.
And possibly most significant for our purposes, Yahweh himself and

not an angelic intermediary touches Jeremiah's lips, and as he does so literally puts his words into Jeremiah's mouth. Yahweh's message goes from his mouth to Jeremiah's via Yahweh's hand, eliminating the need for Yahweh to speak and Jeremiah to hear.

As with his forerunners, so with Ezekiel—the call narrative centers on the message he is to deliver:

"But you, son of man, hear what I say to you; be not rebellious like that rebellious house; open your mouth, and eat what I give you." And when I looked, behold, a hand was stretched out to me, and, lo, a written scroll was in it; and he spread it before me; and it had writing on the front and on the back, and there were written on it words of lamentation and mourning and woe. And he said to me, "Son of man, eat what is offered to you; eat this scroll, and go, speak to the house of Israel." So I opened my mouth, and he gave me the scroll to eat. And said to me, "Son of man, eat this scroll that I give you and fill your stomach with it." Then I ate it; and it was in my mouth as sweet as honey. (Ezek. 2:8–3:3)

Ezekiel is not straightforwardly given words to say (whether by dictation, as with Isaiah, or manually, as with Jeremiah); rather the words are written on a scroll and he is asked to eat the scroll. While this method of communication may seem at first somewhat roundabout, it is used in order to make a very direct point. Yahweh's word is Ezekiel's food. One of the Bible's central themes is that you are what you eat (finding expression, for example, in the Hebrew dietary laws and the Christian eucharist, not to mention the fact that it is a controlling metaphor in any number of biblical texts, like the story of Eve and the fruit and the appeals made by Dame Folly and Madame Wisdom in Prov. 9). Because Ezekiel eats Yahweh's word, he is that word.

Thus, as we go from Isaiah through Jeremiah to Ezekiel we see an intensification of the method Yahweh uses to communicate his word to the prophets. With Jeremiah he is more direct than with Isaiah, with Ezekiel more dramatic. The effect of this intensification is to reduce the distance between prophet and Yahweh's word, a process culminating in what amounts to an identification: prophet is word.

WORD AND EVENT

And now for the third movement, far and away the most difficult to describe. In it word becomes event. In trying to understand how this happens, it is crucial to remember that what is here described as three distinct movements are really indivisible, and moreover, take place more or less simultaneously. Therefore, the word that becomes event is a word already in the process of joining together with the person of the prophet, who in turn is in the process of becoming indistinct from his office. The mechanism by which this word/person/office becomes event seems to be the ever increasing identification of the prophet with the suffering of his people, an identification that gradually becomes mediatory (that is, the prophet does not merely suffer with but for), and finally vicarious.

The prophets crucially involved are Hosea, Jeremiah, and Ezekiel. It is mainly the vicissitudes of Hosea's marriage that reveal both his deep personal identification with his people and also the suffering that this identification entails for him. Significantly, in 2:2–3 we do not at first know that it is Yahweh who is speaking:

> Plead with your mother, plead—
> for she is not my wife,
> and I am not her husband—
> that she put away her harlotry from her face,
> and her adultery from between her breasts;
> lest I strip her naked
> and make her as in the day she was born,
> and make her like a wilderness,
> and set her like a parched land,
> and slay her with thirst.

Of course, we should not read too much into Hosea's marriage. No hint of mediatory suffering is yet present. Nevertheless, Hosea and Gomer and their children are not merely signs but symbols, in the sense that they quite literally participate in the thing symbolized and act it out. They are stand-ins for Yahweh and Israel. (In contrast, Isaiah's children "A Remnant Shall Return" and "The Spoil Speeds, the Prey Hastes" are signs only, for, as far as we are told in the narrative, they neither act out the message their names convey nor participate proleptically in the events referred to.)

Jeremiah is Hosea's true heir, but with a difference. Jeremiah's suffering, unlike Hosea's, comes at the hands of the people, so that instead of participating with them in their suffering, he pictures himself as their sacrificial victim:

> The LORD made it known to me and I knew;
> then thou didst show me their evil deeds.
> But I was like a gentle lamb
> led to the slaughter.
> I did not know it was against me
> they devised schemes. . . .   (Jer. 11:18–19a)

"Gentle lamb" is an image pregnant with consequences for the future, for it leads quite naturally to the idea of the scapegoat. All one need do to accomplish this transition is interpret persecution (suffering because of) as mediation (suffering on behalf of).

In Ezekiel a step is taken in this direction:

And you, O son of man, take a brick and lay it before you, and portray upon it a city, even Jerusalem; and put siegeworks against it. . . . and let it be in a state of siege. . . . Then lie upon your left side, and I will lay the punishment of the house of Israel upon you; for the number of the days that you lie upon it, you shall bear their punishment. . . . And when you have completed these, you shall lie down a second time, but on your right side, and bear the punishment of the house of Judah. . . .   (Ezek. 4:1–4, 6)

As von Rad says, "Here is something much more than the realistic demonstration of a tremendous guilt: it is the imposition of this guilt on one man whose task it is to bear it."[3]   And yet, Ezekiel's suffering is not yet vicarious in the full sense of that term.   That is, no statement is made that Israel, by virtue of Ezekiel's suffering, will escape suffering, or that Ezekiel's suffering is the means of Israel's forgiveness and redemption.

THE SERVANT AND JESUS

Before proceeding to the final two episodes in the plot of God's word become both person and event, it may be well to sum up where we are.   With Ezekiel, as a result of a gradual process begun with Amos and Hosea, a process fueled by the partial inadequacy of the spoken prophetic word, the first two movements described above are virtually complete: person is united with office and word with person. This person/word/office has not yet, however, become the saving event itself, although it is close.

It is left for Yahweh's servant described for us in the writings of Second Isaiah to continue the first two movements and complete the third:

Surely he has borne our griefs
    and carried our sorrows;
yet we esteemed him stricken,
    smitten by God, and afflicted.
But he was wounded for our transgressions,
    he was bruised for our iniquities;
upon him was the chastisement that made us whole
    and with his stripes we are healed.
All we like sheep have gone astray;
    we have turned every one to his own way;
and the LORD has laid on him
    the iniquity of us all.   (Isa. 53:4–6)

3. Von Rad, *Old Testament Theology*, vol. II, p. 275.

Note, first, that person has become so absorbed into office that the servant has no personality apart from his office. In fact, he has no personal name; he is known only by his title, servant of Yahweh. Note, second, that word has been so absorbed into person that the servant says nothing! What he accomplishes is his word. And, finally, observe that his is truly vicarious suffering: his death is the saving event. In short, person, office, word, and event are one.

It would seem, then, that our plot has reached its climax. Surprisingly, however, the servant is actually an anticlimax. The problem is that the salvation he achieves, or, we might more appropriately say, the salvation he is, is efficacious for none of the parties in our story, except possibly for the "we" who speak Isaiah 53, and their identity is unknown. Outside of Second Isaiah the servant and his great accomplishment are not even acknowledged. Consequently, what seems at first glance to be the fulfillment of prophecy ironically turns into one more prophecy whose fulfillment is looked for in the future; what seems to be word become event turns out to be a word only.

It remains for Jesus of Nazareth to fulfill this prophecy, to be the word become truly event, or, as the Bible puts it, to be the word made flesh:

In the beginning was the Word, and the Word was with God, and the Word was God. He was in the beginning with God; all things were made through him, and without him was not anything made that was made. In him was life, and the life was the light of men. . . . And the Word became flesh and dwelt among us, full of grace and truth; we have beheld his glory, glory as of the only Son from the Father. (John 1:1-4, 14)

In Genesis 1 God spoke and it was so; that is, word and event were so united that the mere speaking of the word brought into being the event referred to. Never again in the Old Testament is the connection between word and event so close. To be sure, God's word generally becomes event, but the process may take a few centuries, as with his words to Abraham. Eventually, the distance between word and event is so great, as with promises of a glorious restoration of the nation Israel, that the prophets attempt to reunite them. Their efforts are completed in Jesus, who once again speaks and it is so. His life, death, and resurrection are a word that re-creates the world for those who speak their belief in him; they become new creations. Furthermore, his word brings into being a new community out of the old and this community and their leaders now replace Abraham's community as the major subject of the remainder of the biblical narrative.

81

POETS AS PROPHETS

If we turn now from considering the Bible as one grand book to a consideration of the whole of Western literature as one grand masterpiece, we can in a sense see a continuation of the biblical saga of word and event, with the term poet (meaning, in this context, any writer of pure literature) replacing that of prophet. I can here, of course, do no more than delineate the bare outlines of the plot.

The Christian word, or the word-event spoken by Jesus, is by and large taken as valid by Western poets up until, roughly, the Renaissance, just as God's word to Moses was counted valid by the Israelite nation up to the rise of Assyria and Babylonia. Hence their words, somewhat analogous to the words of prophets like Elijah and Elisha, needed only to describe that reality, or apply it in various cultural settings. However, during the Renaissance, not because of the invasion of foreign enemies, but because of the invasion of science and its allies, the Christian word was increasingly called into question. Finally, a time came when the discrepancy between the Christian description of reality and the description given in scientific theories became so great that a new word was needed.

And just as Amos and company arose to speak a new word to Israel, the romantic poets[4] arose as latter-day prophets to speak a new word to the Western world. They were the first group of poets to realize in a thoroughgoing way that the Christian word had lost its explaining and consoling power for their contemporaries, and to set about more or less self-consciously to replace it with alternative symbolic structures. They faced squarely the claim by science that its methods alone give access to truth, a claim that would mean that truth resides in a nature bereft of human values. In response, they postulated the thoroughly human poetic imagination and believed that it either created a transcendent realm of Beauty and Truth or acted as a mediator between mankind and such a spiritual realm.

Romantic notions of the exalted role of the poet are most eloquently put in Shelley's *A Defence of Poetry*. Because the poet "participates in the eternal, the infinite and the one," he can be both prophet and legislator: "he not only beholds intensely the present as it is, and discovers those laws according to which present things ought to be ordered, but he beholds the future in the present, and his thoughts

---

4. While I believe that this analysis is essentially valid for most, if not all, Western cultures, I will limit my remarks to British and American poets, with whom I am most familiar.

are the germs of the flower and fruit of latest time." He ends his *Defence* with the famous lines:

Poets are the hierophants of an unapprehended inspiration; the mirrors of the gigantic shadows which futurity casts upon the present; the words which express what they understand not; the trumpets which sing to battle, and feel not what they inspire; the influence which is moved not, but moves. Poets are the unacknowledged legislators of the world.[5]

In line with this notion of the poetic office, and corresponding to Old Testament prophetic visions of a new order, Blake wrote his prophecies of the resurrection of Albion (that is, England) and of the building of "Jerusalem/In England's green and pleasant Land" (Preface to "Milton"); Wordsworth sang the spousal verse for the coming wedding of man's mind to the "goodly universe" (Preface to *The Excursion*); Keats recast the classical myth of the fall of the Titans (in *Hyperion* and *The Fall of Hyperion*); and Shelley dreamed of a society based on love and justice (in, for example, *Prometheus Unbound*). The visions of these poets, however, did not materialize in history. Their words, too, like those of their Old Testament counterparts, proved discrepant from reality.

The response of the community of poets to this situation is directly comparable to the response of the Old Testament prophets. That is, in the first place, they tried, as in the symbolist movement, to make their words not merely point to a visionary world but embody it. Somehow, the words of the poem incarnated the world of Beauty and Truth. And, in the second place, they tried so to identify with their office as poet that they would embody in themselves the visionary world. They would be, as it were, secular incarnations. Hence, the extraordinary preoccupation of many nineteenth and twentieth century poets with finding a life style commensurate with their high office. The poet, both in the poem and in life, becomes his own hero.

And the story of the word incarnate is today still being told by poets like Allen Ginsberg, many of whose poems (like *Wichita Vortex Sutra*) are enactments of the creative poetic word, and whose actions in society (as at the Democratic convention in Chicago in 1968) reflect the notion of the poet as the suffering servant. Perhaps this story will never end so long as there are poets to tell and audiences to listen!

---

5. P. B. Shelley, *Selected Poems, Essays, and Letters*, ed. Ellsworth Barnard (New York: Odyssey Press, 1944), p. 568.

THE BIBLE AS LITERATURE (REPRISE)

The God of the Bible is the poet par excellence. Not only does he by his word create the world, but by embodying his word in a man he restores that now fallen world and offers to every human being the possibility of a full and significant life. If the above analysis has any merit, it is not perhaps too great an exaggeration to say that some poets imitate God's creation while others do no less than imitate God himself. That is, they attempt to create a new world by the imaginative use of language. The prophets belong to this latter group, as do their true heirs in the Western literary tradition, poets like William Blake, Percy Bysshe Shelley, William Butler Yeats, Walt Whitman, and Wallace Stevens. As the last named says of a solitary woman singing beside the ocean at Key West, a woman who functions in the poem as a symbol of the poet:

> She was the single artificer of the world
> In which she sang. And when she sang, the sea,
> Whatever self it had, became the self
> That was her song, for she was the maker. Then we,
> As we beheld her striding there alone,
> Knew that there never was a world for her
> Except the one she sang and, singing, made.[6]

Of course, for the poet to be effective, we must, again in the words of Wallace Stevens, "receive his poetry" ("The Noble Rider and the Sound of Words"), that is, we must read his words and by an act of our own imagination enter into the world those words create. The process is analogous to religious conversion. Interestingly enough, then, if the Bible as literature is read in this way, its essential function remains, formally speaking, the same as when it is read as sacred scripture: in both cases it is a word addressed to a hearer and requires an imaginative response on his part before it can be fully entered into and understood. However, and here is the rub, the Bible as literature is fiction. Its dramatis personae are imitations of real people, its actions imitations of real actions, and its thoughts imitations of real thoughts (see Chapter I). Therefore, its power as literature is hardly what its power as scripture is. To return to Robert Frost's statement quoted at the conclusion of Chapter I, a poem "ends in a clarification of life—not necessarily a great clarification, such as sects and cults are founded on, but in a momentary stay against confusion" ("The Figure a Poem Makes").

6. Wallace Stevens, "The Idea of Order at Key West," *The Collected Poems of Wallace Stevens* (New York: Alfred A. Knopf, 1968), pp. 128–30.

So the Bible as literature is not so powerful as the Bible as scripture. But that's all right. The fact, from the point of view of many readers, that literature is not capable of granting ultimate clarifications is a blessing and part of its tragic grandeur. It is so wonderful, this rhythmic ordering of words, and yet, with regard to the real world, the world of international conflicts, of global fear, of pain and suffering, of individual anxiety and indecision, it can do so little. "Poetry makes nothing happen," says Auden ("In Memory of W. B. Yeats"). To be so full and yet so empty! No wonder so many people have turned to literature for clarification and consolation. And if we consider the Bible's focus and range, and the resolving power of the lens through which it presents the human spectacle, no wonder that these same people have adopted it into their canon of the supreme masterpieces of the human imagination.

Bibliographical Essay

The most direct and reliable way to learn the discipline of literary criticism is to read literature, as much of it as possible, beginning with the Greeks and continuing to the 1970s, and encompassing all genres and most of the languages of the Western world. Since time and interest will force most readers to be selective, the following books are offered as a basic reading list. Choice of these particular volumes is, of course, heavily influenced by the literary perspective that informs this book:

Homer, *Iliad* and *Odyssey*
Aeschylus, *Oresteia*
Sophocles, *Oedipus the King* and *Oedipus at Colonus*
Euripides, *The Bacchae* and *Medea*
Aristophanes, *Clouds, Birds,* and *Frogs*
Dante, *The Divine Comedy*
Shakespeare, *King Lear, The Tempest,* and *Henry IV*
Milton, *Paradise Lost*
Blake, *Marriage of Heaven and Hell* and *Jerusalem*
Wordsworth, *The Prelude*
Keats, "The Great Odes"
Whitman, "Song of Myself"
Yeats, *The Collected Poems of W. B. Yeats*
Eliot, *Collected Poems*
Frost, *Complete Poems of Robert Frost*
Stevens, *The Collected Poems of Wallace Stevens*

As companions to these books the classics of literary criticism should be read. The following are two excellent anthologies: H. Adams, *Critical Theory Since Plato* (New York: Harcourt Brace Jovanovich, 1971) and a two-volume paperback set, A. H. Gilbert, *Literary Criticism, Plato to Dryden* (Detroit: Wayne State University Press, 1962) and G. W. Allen and H. H. Clark, *Literary Criticism, Pope to Croce* (Detroit: Wayne State University Press, 1962). L. I. Lipking and A. W. Litz, *Modern Literary Criticism* (New York: Atheneum, 1972) is an adequate anthology of modern literary criticism. Its selections from the critical writings of T. S. Eliot and Ezra Pound are excellent, but one would be well advised to omit the chapters on I. A. Richards and Northrop Frye and go directly to Richards, *Principles of Literary Criticism* (New York: Harcourt, Brace & World, 1925) and *Practical Criticism* (New York: Harcourt, Brace & World, 1929) and N. Frye, *Anatomy of Criticism* (Princeton: Princeton University Press,

1957). There is little doubt that Frye's book is the single most important volume of literary criticism for students of the Bible.

Other books of criticism that are likely to be helpful to biblical critics are K. Burke, *The Philosophy of Literary Form* (Baton Rouge: Louisiana State University Press, 1941); M. Krieger, *The New Apologists for Poetry* (Minneapolis: University of Minnesota Press, 1956), an insightful summary of literary critical debate during the first half of this century, and *A Window to Criticism* (Princeton: Princeton University Press, 1964), which contains an extraordinary discussion of the relation of poem to reality; J. H. Miller, *Poets of Reality* (Cambridge: Harvard University Press, 1966), an in-depth discussion of the religious and philosophical implications of the works of Eliot, Yeats, Thomas, Stevens, and Williams; and F. Kermode, *The Sense of an Ending* (New York: Oxford, 1967), a study of narrative fiction in light of the theory of fictions as espoused by such people as Wallace Stevens.

Literary criticism of biblical texts is still in its infancy. Most of the work done in the past decade or so is to be found in journals. *Semeia* and *Linguistica Biblica* are devoted almost exclusively to literary and linguistic studies of biblical materials. Two pioneering efforts in this field that are still worthy of attention are R. G. Moulton, *The Literary Study of the Bible* (Boston: D. C. Heath & Co., 1895), and D. B. McDonald, *The Hebrew Literary Genius* (Princeton: Princeton University Press, 1933). Among more recent studies L. Alonso-Schökel, *The Inspired Word* (New York: Herder & Herder, 1965), and E. M. Good, *Irony in the Old Testament* (Philadelphia: Westminster Press, 1965), stand out both in terms of the excellence of their presentations and in terms of their influence on other scholars. E. Auerbach, *Mimesis* (Princeton University Press, 1953), contains a justly famous interpretation of Hebrew narrative style in its first chapter, entitled "Odysseus' Scar." And, finally, K. R. R. Gros Louis. J. S. Ackerman, and T. S. Warshaw, eds., *Literary Interpretations of Biblical Narratives* (Nashville: Abingdon Press, 1974), contains some instructive literary analyses of selected biblical texts.